Dat

THE POWER OF FREEDOM

THE POWER OF

FREEDOM

BY MAX ASCOLI

FARRAR, STRAUS AND COMPANY · NEW YORK

ff

Manufactured in the U.S.A.

By J. J. Little and Ives Company, New York

Designed by Stefan Salter

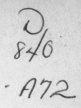

TO PETE
MY SON

CONTENTS

INTRODUCTION

In writing this book I have aimed to prove two points: 1) In the present world political struggle the democratic position is far stronger than we know; 2) Both our awareness and our use of this strength are dangerously hampered by the fact that our thinking about democracy has grown obsolete and cliché-ridden. In other words, among the many things which are wrong in our world one of the most wrong lies in our minds—in the minds of the people who in the present political struggle stand for freedom.

Wrongs of the mind are of a particularly sticky nature and cannot be overcome by pulling ourselves up by the bootstraps of our good intentions and avowals of guilt. Yet there is no reason why an effort should not be made to cope with them, even if, as in the case of this particular effort, it results in the presentation of a book of ideas. Books of ideas are not notably welcomed in this day and place. As to ideas themselves, they have come to acquire a position like that of garlic in our gastronomic habits: a trifle lends flavor to a salad, but a mouthful gives you a revolting breath.

Yet, if I may use a half-trite, half-humiliating argument, ideas are of terrific importance in our time. No matter what their content is or what they are called—freedom (one freedom or four), national independence, proletarian revolution or master race—these tools that the mind devises to cope with a complex reality and make a dent in it have exerted an appalling influence on the life of men. Many an ideological germ, cultivated for laboratory purposes or just for fun, has run wild in our time and blighted the world.

Perhaps it is out of a healthy, half-conscious awareness of the seditious character of ideas that the Anglo-Saxon countries have shown a tendency to impose a sort of birth control on them. Clichés are safer and can do as well— clichés about rights, which are, of course, "inalienable," no matter what use men make of them; about the human person which is "sacred," no matter what has happened in these last years to quite a few bearers of this sacredness; and about freedom which, you know, is not quite "perfect," even here, but just compare it with what other people have.

This method might work if the Anglo-Saxon peoples were living in such complete isolation that they were immune from the spread or the consequences of ideological blights. Unfortunately, the method does not work, even in America, a nation that has tried to cultivate its own immunity by quarantining ideas, checking their reproduction and grinding them into pulp, to meet what is supposed to be popular demand.

That the method does not work, even for America, is evidenced by the fact that twice in a generation American might has had to be mobilized because the reality of total war had failed to respect its isolation. In our day it is indisputable that only the wise use of American power and resources can bring some sanity and order into the world. But while Americans are legitimately hurt whenever they are told that they cannot contribute anything but power and resources (dollars), they are extremely ill at ease whenever it is up to them to make workable for foreign peoples the principles for which America stands.

As if they were philosopher-kings, American statesmen are constantly asked at international conferences what they mean by democracy and popular rights. Their stammering answers bear witness to the fact that if the world is in desperate need of American goods, it can scarcely use the American method of dealing with ideas. Yet America too has a desperate need: to let the world know that she has something to contribute besides dollars.

My contention is that America has this something; that each of our basic principles—freedom, rights, the worth of the human person, national independence—is justified and founded on formidable truths which the needs of our time have made unquestionable. Even on the ground of sheer efficiency these principles are infinitely superior to any put forward by competing ideologies. But all these truths and all their usefulness come to nothing if the principles get rusty, defaced by sloganized repetition and withered by fundamentalism—as we have allowed them to do. The political principles that give character to our society should always be kept one step ahead of the course of economics and technology, in order to exert some control over them. But in an era of supersonic speed our political ideas are trotting along at the restful pace of the horse and buggy.

From what precedes, the reader will gather that this is a profoundly optimistic book. It is optimistic because it is based on the assumption that our system of values is stronger than we think—indeed, stronger than we deserve. It is optimistic because it is impatient with all the loud chatter about the end of civilization, the passing of the era of freedom, the need of some kind of thoroughgoing, all-upsetting revolution. I do not think we need revolution; but what we do need is to be more thoroughly aware of the values for which we stand.

Finally, this book is optimistic because it is predicated on the belief that what is wrong in our minds can be cured by reason in our minds. The book, of course, does not pretend to offer a cure, but it does try to point out a direction, to suggest a course, and to back up the suggestion with some measure of example.

In writing a book of this kind, I had a difficult choice to make. I could have tried to write what is called a scientific book, discussing the various points with great authorities who are dead and with influential ones who are alive. Or I could have made the book a long and discursive one, jammed with references to the facts of today and of yesterday, in order to justify the theories I wanted to propose. Then there was the third solution: to concentrate the analysis of the most compelling facts of our day in the early portions and let the ideas stand or fall on their own merits. This is the solution I finally adopted. The other two had their worth, but I think the issues I try to raise are too serious and urgent to be confronted from behind a bookcase or a stack of newspaper clippings.

However, the writing of a book of this kind obviously presupposes a certain theoretical and literary background. The reader who cares to will have no difficulty in finding out the current of thought to which I belong. To help those who might care, I name the important theorists who, with no responsibility of their own, have influenced the ideas developed here.

Starting, as we always must, with the Greeks, Aristotle's thinking has certainly influenced me more than Plato's, and the stoic over any Greek-Roman school of thought. Perhaps my most conscious indebtedness is to Italian political philosophy: Dante, Machiavelli, and above all, Vico, to whose thinking I have been exposed so thoroughly and unreservedly for so many years that I constantly realize how I follow Vico even when I think I have forgotten him. To some extent, this applies to Croce too. I think I have been constantly moving away from his influence, but as a grown-up man moves away from his family.

There is no hiding the fact that I love Burke and loathe Rousseau. Among American political thinkers, the writers of *The Federalist* are high at the top, with Hamilton second to none. When it comes to nineteenth-century social reformers, there is no love lost for Marx and Engels, while Proudhon and Sorel stirred me early in my life. Of the political writers of the last century, the one whose work I have most admired and cherished is De Tocqueville.

I thus submit my identification papers bearing some great names that I use not as reference, but to assist those who may wish to pigeonhole my book. This is a legitimate demand of the reader and I have no reason to claim exemption on the ground that I have written a book without footnotes.

The author of a book on politics has no right to squirm when an attempt is made to give him a political label. Rather he should take a hand in his own labeling. I am a liberal, and I don't want to add any qualifying adjective. In spite of the way this word has been abused, it is still good enough for me. I believe that freedom, as the title of this book suggests, is the propulsive power of civilization—a power that men have the ability to release and to control. I also believe that this power can drive the men of our time to goals so high and so good that we can only dimly discern them.

To develop this conception of freedom and to relate it to the specific facts and the emerging institutions of our day, this book has been written.

PART I

THE WORLD CIVIL WAR

CHAPTER I

THE SHADOW OF COMMUNISM

"A specter is haunting Europe—the specter of
Communism." (*Communist Manifesto* 1848).

AFTER a hundred years communism has lost nothing
of its ghostlike quality. Everywhere we see this shadow
that we call communism caricaturing in distorted reflec-
tions the patterns of our institutions and our beliefs. The
constantly shifting lines of its "democracy," its "united
fronts," its "anti-fascism," pursue whatever we do to further democracy and popular unity or to counter fascism.
Even our own identity is confused, for those who believe
in freedom as the best that can be made of life are constantly trailed by those who sneer at freedom and yet
claim to be its guardian.

Communism has a corrosive quality. When it gets hold
of a man, it erases kindness from his face. The hardened
features become a thick mask that cuts all communication
between the life inside a man and what lies outside him.
Wherever it appears, it exhibits the same traits: it confuses
issues, it embitters conflicts, it breeds a spirit of suspicion
and fanaticism that calls for more suspicion and fanaticism. It wants to make scared fanatics of all of us. It

3

bedevils its opponents into becoming what it thinks they are, in order that its notion of man and of history may be verified.

This century-old disorder reached its acute stage when Soviet Russia gave to abstruse dogmas the support of a hard, practical reality. Since that time, the bedevilment of communism's opponents has not been left to chance. It has become systematic, thorough, unremitting, with as many facets as there are tender spots in the anti-communist world. It is all oriented toward one goal: to keep its opponents constantly harassed and constantly on the defensive. As long as the anti-communists are on the defensive, hard-pressed to justify their record and their belief, as long as the offensive is steady and relentless, then even the sordid features of communist life in Soviet Russia can be obscured and made alluring.

The fact is that the Soviet economy, far from abolishing business cycles, has replaced them with so-called purges, where miscalculations on the part of holders of economic power are horribly punished in the ever-spreading persecution of "saboteurs." And certainly no process of capital accumulation in the countries of the West, at the cost of uprooted peasants, underpaid workers or colonial natives, was ever so cruel as that of Soviet Russia where peasants were famished by the millions, workers deprived of trade union rights and masses of men and women reduced to the abjection of slavery.

Yet the communist offensive could proceed relentlessly for two reasons. The first is that the economic and political consolidation of the Soviet regime imitated, with an extraordinarily cruel vengeance, patterns and abuses that the capitalistic nations had established or tolerated. The second reason is that communist aggressiveness found a response in every capitalistic or democratic country in which democracy's promises had not been fulfilled and democratic thinking had grown sluggish.

According to the *Communist Manifesto*, the growth of our political and economic order should create the conditions that make communism inevitable. But in these hundred years, every one of the trends that was supposed to lead to this inevitable end has led the opposite way. Not one of the events that the writers of the *Communist Manifesto* prophesied has come to pass as predicted. It is not true that the process of industrialism leads to the increasing misery and subjection of the workers—except perhaps in Soviet Russia. It is not true that technology irreparably destroys the independence or the privacy of the small community and the family. For it has been proved over and over again that the wounds inflicted on society by technology can be healed by technology—as the farmer and the remote producer learned when their mode of living, threatened by the steam engine, was infinitely enriched by the paved road, the diesel motor and electric power.

It has been proved beyond any possible doubt that it is simply not true that the most economically and technologically advanced countries are the ripest for communism. It is not true that communism is the natural and inevitable result of capitalism or of capitalistic democracy. The lie to these prophecies has been given by the fact that communism has been established not in the most but in the least developed countries, not as an inevitable result of industrialism but as a man-willed and man-conducted experiment in inevitability—spurred by the police state.

Yet democrats have been no less hard pressed because

communist doctrines have failed and history has given the lie to communist prophecies. On the contrary, communist attacks have become more aggressive the more dismal the communist failures. It is as if democracy and capitalism were held responsible for these failures, as if it were their fault that communism had to start with the most unprogressive, underdeveloped countries. And perhaps to a very large extent this is true; democracy is responsible for communism, because communism is not an outgrowth of technology and democracy, but rather of democracy's inability to grow with the growth of technology and make the proper use of it.

The shadow of communism gives us an uneasy conscience. Communist thinking is a distortion of our modes of economic and political thinking. Its practices can always find a precedent that has been established by us. Thus communism shamelessly fakes elections, brings people from their graves to vote and stuffs the ballots. But not even these tactics are original since, in perhaps more decent forms, they were part of the political tradition of the democracies.

Our relationship with communism can be settled neither by agreement nor by war with Soviet Russia, neither by toleration nor by persecution of the communist outposts within our borders. Just because it is a disorder of our conscience, it is our own problem that we have to settle with ourselves: why are we so disturbed by communism, why is its threat, no matter how remote, always likely to make us lose our poise and sometimes even the sense of our own interest?

What we share with communism upsets us much more

than what divides us from it. The peace of the world and
our own democracy are only relatively endangered by the
wide gulf stretched between the Russian and the democratic modes of living. The world has survived even greater
ideological or religious differences, and the more we know
about life in communist countries, the better we realize
the inner soundness of our democratic order. Much more
disturbing is the fact that we have still in common with
the communists not only political habits and practices,
but some of the fundamental tenets on which the fabric
of our society rests.

We rely on technology as on the mainspring of social
progress; we are accustomed to have party organizations
established side by side with those of the state; we have no
doubts that the individual rate of production and consumption is the best possible index of human well-being. Communism has eagerly adopted all these fundamental tenets.
It makes a fetish of all the technological and political tools
that have been devised to regulate the behavior of men;
with its five-year plans it relentlessly prods the output
of production and makes the attainment of certain pre-
figured quotas into a supreme and even glorious social ideal.
It has no scruples in subordinating the welfare of the people
under its rule to the overriding claims of the political and
of the technological managers.

All this sounds ghastly to us, and at the same time familiar, like the deliberate repetition on a gigantic scale of
things we have been doing hesitantly and piecemeal. At
times, the difference between communism and our own
order seems to be one of quantity more than of quality, of
manners more than of substance. It is against our nature
to consider men as entirely subordinate to their machinery
of production and of government. But where can we find

the boundary line in between what these machineries can and what they cannot ask of men? How can we check the trend that both industrialism and bureaucracy have unleashed? How can we control the economic and political power that we have learned to release and that we think we need?

Sometimes the dismal thought hits our mind that, in spite of its unfulfilled prophecies and absurd doctrines, communism may be what the years to come have in store for us, and that perhaps its leaders are the abominable forerunners of an abominable future. For sometimes we fear that neither the institutions of personal liberty nor those of national freedom are strong enough to stop a trend that seems to be sweeping all over the world and that leads to the complete subordination of man to his own technological and political instruments. This fear makes for strife and war—a particularly devastating war, since its main battlefield is inside ourselves.

For centuries, a world civil war has been in the making that has finally exploded at the end of the first World War. It is not primarily marked by ideological issues or by the conflict between opposite systems of social or political organization. Rather, it is marked, on one side, by our yearning for freedom that we do not know how to readjust to the new conditions of the world and by the tendency, on the other side, to gleefully accept the total subjection of men on a world-wide scale to the mechanisms that their technological and political ingenuity has devised. For men do not seem to have the capacity to put adequate brakes to the power they have learned to release. If, instead of casual contenders, there were real parties in the world civil war, they could be called the party of the brakes and the party of the inevitable.

Communism is the closest approximation to the party of
the inevitable. It is more than doubtful whether it is our
future, unless we resign ourselves to it, but certainly it is
the diligently collected, assiduously cultivated sum total
of the mistakes and failures of our past. It constantly bedevils us with its maddening echoes of our emptiest slogans
and devitalized ideas. It harps on our bad conscience and
on our mental laziness. It insists that, no matter what we
do, its final victory is a foregone conclusion. We protest in
vain that perhaps something of it comes from us, but that
it is our caricature and that we are entirely different from
it. Quoting facts, we give it the lie. Appealing to reason,
we prove its absurdity. Yet we cannot shake it loose.

Nor can we beat it at its own game by organizing our
own fellow-travelers and cells and party lines. We are no
match for communism in a game of deception and ruthlessness, and if in order to destroy communism we adopt
its totalitarianism, we lose our own identity. Our relationship with communism is so close, the hold it has on us is
so strong, that we are in constant danger of totally dis-
figuring ourselves when, threatened or exasperated, we
hit back at it. If to fight it we adopt communist patterns—
a one-party system, compulsory discipline of labor and
unanimous elections—that is the end of us. Then the efforts
to wrestle with the long-drawn projection of our errors
carries us to that mad, suicidal frenzy that is fascism.

Not even the final crushing of fascism and the supreme
evidence of valor that the free nations have given to themselves, not even this seemed to have been enough to re-
establish our self-confidence. For the nervous disorder is
still here—the dizziness which is waiting for us at whatever height we climb, the obsession that whatever we do,
whatever new weapon or tool our ingenuity may discover

is going to boomerang against us. For there are no checks against what we do. This dizziness, this obsession of our minds, is communism—not Soviet Russia, not the miserable communist intriguers in our midst.

There are quite a few people in our times who because of this nervous disorder live from day to day, from one international or national crisis to another, as if they were on temporary leave from doom. Doom, of course, is just another name for communism.

The loudest warnings of doom were heard just at the end of the war, when it became known that man could release atomic energy for his own purposes. Far from being stirred by the creative possibilities of atomic power, we could think only of the infinite misery of its use for total destruction.

The controlled release of atomic energy promises relief from the nightmare of exhausting the main sources of physical energy upon which our civilization depends. At the same time it is bound to make further and deeper inroads into the privileges of those nations which, until now, have been the most fortunate and the most powerful. Like every other form of energy, and as the most prodigious of them all, it is destined to equalize the opportunities of peoples.

Here we see power in its most formidable and compelling form, its source, its effect and its possibilities for use. Power is equal to our capacity to use it. Once this capacity is organized and its rules, the mode of its acquisition formulated, it enters into the patrimony of the human race. What is contained under the dome of a human skull receives a mold there that makes it accessible to other human

minds. Because the production of atomic energy is imitable
—despite the awesomeness and complexity of its initial
apparatus—it will become increasingly simple, more teachable and more usable.

A greater equalization of power is bound to follow. This
is the trend, the way of all man-made power: the greater
its effectiveness, the more inevitable its popularization;
the greater its range, the more irrevocable its liberating
influence.

The skills of generations past are put at the disposal of
living man so that the effectiveness of his acts, the reach
of his hands, may be prodigiously increased. These skills
teach man to be increasingly obedient to nature, to establish co-operation with it, that he may use for his own
purposes some of the untold energies of which nature is
made. These energies would have remained forever stored,
these secrets forever hidden, were it not for the human
mind that establishes links and co-relations and imposes
its will.

The human mind has been evolving during three thousand years of Greek-Hebrew-Christian civilization. We
would not now have such teachable, simplified forms of
ever-greater power, if principles of communication among
men had not been established according to the exact rules
of science; and the patrimony of science could not have
been augmented from generation to generation, if our
particular heritage had not made of man's mind a vessel in
which human experience could be deposited, reassembled
and transmitted.

After so much sowing, this should be a time of glorious
harvesting. Instead we see it as a day fraught with disaster.
In our new release of power we seem able to see only

potential evil. It is said on all sides that here is a power too great for man to bear.

This is a cowardly, dishonorable thing to say. It is as cowardly as another saying is trite: that every new discovery, every new power granted to man, increases his potentiality for evil. We should say, rather, that every new discovery sharpens man's realization of the cleavage between good and evil, gives to good and evil more and more compelling features of unmistakable reality. Every new discovery makes the choice between good and evil less of a choice, if man is not afraid of choosing.

Every grant of power energizes man's will to survival. At the same time, each new accession of power gives to evil a self-denouncing, all-pervading impact. We have just seen in Hitler the embodiment of evil for our time.

This latest grant of power gives our generation a chance to direct the lives of men toward a level of well-being never before conceived of. Instead, the thought that Communist Russia might some day use atomic energy has been enough to unloose in us a gigantic wave of fear. Men rushed to figure out how the political order of the world could be changed without delay, regardless of what might happen to the freedom of the individual or of nations. Other men suggested that if a docile Russia did not immediately enter a new universal order, then war had better come soon, with Russia as the target. For we seem to think of atom bombs as the only cure for our fear and our nervous disorder.

Adolf Hitler, from his unmarked grave, must suffer the anguish of envy. The democracies have found a way to rush the process over which he labored so hard. They can go now, through fear of communism, to total and irretrievable ruin, on a scale greater and with results more thorough than his mad mind could ever have dreamed.

CHAPTER II

LEST WE FORGET HIM

HITLER'S DEATH may prove to have been more calamitous than his life, if we do not focus our minds on what he did to us. He was the one who, by threatening our very existence, showed us the road to survival. He was the one who showed us what happens to a nation that adopts totalitarianism in order to stop communism.

We did not need him, and the price of what we have learned or achieved because of him has been unbearably high; but we need to summon his memory and keep it alive, in order that we may not have to pay an even higher price for failing to prevent a recurrence of the blight that we called by the name of Adolf Hitler. We cannot afford to let him go, to escape the wrath of the living at his own will. No matter what has actually happened to him we cannot afford to rely on his death, accepting as a fact that he vanished from the earth in a cloud of fire and smoke.

Most of what he destroyed has remained destroyed. The millions of human lives he extinguished have not regained their existence with his disappearance; the institutions, the political principles he violated, are still as flattened as when he ran over them; and the examples he set

will not be erased until each one of them becomes a standard measure of ruthlessly punishable crime.

For there is one thing he did that his disappearance must
not be allowed to undo. He convinced us, while he lived,
of the existence of evil as something definite, unadulterated,
unmistakable. He showed us where, and under what conditions, evil in our time has the best chance to grow. If, one
by one, we follow the course of Hitler's struggles, if we
analyze the institutions he attacked and the causes that
made for their ruin, we will have a complete chart of all
the gangrenous spots in our civilization.

Hitler taught us that war is political in its causes and in
its aims, that warfare is a continuation of politics and
politics a softening and dilution of warfare. This was by
no means new, but mankind does not learn its lessons from
books; it reaches its wisdom at the cost of its flesh. It was
comfortable to rest quietly on the assumption that there is
an absolute distinction between the game of politics, national or international, and the game of war; between what
is called peace, with all its trappings of diplomacy, and
what is called war, with all its horrors. Ingenuous as well
as disingenuous men at various times could even believe
that the boundary line between war and peace had been
crossed by mankind once and forever.

Hitler taught us that war and politics can be used as two
allied techniques in the war of nerves, that both of them
can be handled at the same time to twist, harass and break
down the nerves of men. Nations and states are not meta-
physical entities. They are made up of men, and men can
easily be molded when reduced to frightened bundles of

nerves. It was Hitler who reminded us that war is at the foundation of both national and international politics, the dreadful core of it, and that the bloodless technique of politics, although used to exorcise and divert violence, is closely patterned after that of war.

Hitler's secret weapon was his political warfare. The secret was the use of his enemies' internal politics as a weapon of war, and war as an instrument of pressure politics against his enemies. In doing so, he took full advantage of all the conventions of international politics. From the time that national states were organized, the demarcation between domestic and external politics had been considered a boundary line that no self-respecting statesman or politician would cross. Along this boundary line there were large stretches of no man's land, a wild game preserve marked off for the ceremonial fox hunting of diplomats and for the blazing of smugglers' trails.

Hitler settled himself firmly in that area and widened the secret trails into comfortable roads over which his technicians in insurrection as well as arms could be safely imported into the countries he had marked for conquest. Yet when the moment of reckoning was at hand and his conquests ripe, he was quick to adopt as camouflage many of the doctrines which the great democratic powers had regarded as their own. The theory of self-determination protected his march into Austria and the Sudetenland. Under the shelter of the doctrine of non-intervention he fought his war in Spain. The humanitarian necessity of preserving public order in a disintegrating neighboring country paved the way to Prague. One by one, Hitler used all these theories and exploded them. He settled himself on the boundary line between national and international politics, just as he set himself on the line between war and peace.

When military warfare actually started in the fall of 1939, Hitler was ready for some bolder trespassing jaunts. During the first World War the principle of national sovereignty had been redefined by President Wilson according to the democratic dogma: any people who so chose was free to organize its independence within boundaries determined by race, language or history; and independence made of each state a little world in itself, ruled by its own internal politics, and absolute master of its destiny.

All the little sovereign worlds of continental Europe were in line at the beginning of this war. And all but a few of them fell. It was a series of mopping-up operations, timely, and skillfully executed. Everywhere in Europe internal politics, by shriveling and wearing away the roots of every country, had acted as a weapon of Hitler's warfare. All these rivulets of rotting politics were flowing in the same direction, heedless of the boundaries which were to make the sovereign worlds inviolable. Hitler had only to accelerate the flow here and there.

He was perhaps the best wrecker the world has ever known and he appeared at a moment when unparalleled wrecking jobs were at hand. By destroying the democratic order is his own country he had made the German state a headquarters of international subversion. Under the protection of German national sovereignty he had made of his own party an army set to devastate the world. He used and exploded the typical democratic institution called political party in order to abolish all parties and outlaw political competition—just as he used and exploded the world-wide institution called national state in order to write off national states and do away with their peaceful co-existence.

Armed with the tools that modern technology and modern democracy had created, Hitler became the total wrecker, the embodiment of total evil that only our times could produce. He became more than a destroyer of rules, a trespasser of sacred boundaries, a challenger of silent assumptions; he drove beyond constitutional structures and age-old laws of international community. He not only wrecked all these but scorched the earth on which they rested, for he ground them down to the ultimate material of which they are made—the nerves of men. He knew how to atomize the social fabric and how to split that atom.

Hitler knew early in his career that by making internal political tension unbearable, by mutiplying the occasions of conflict—of elections or plebescites—it is possible to reduce the citizens of a democracy to such a condition of confusion and weariness that political freedom loses its meaning and can be taken away from them.

He knew that the best way to cultivate neglect of politics in the bulk of the citizenry is to create a condition of turmoil where their whole lives depend on political decisions that are asked of them and that they are in no condition to make. He knew that the best way to make of the political animal a beast of prey or to break him to the yoke is to force him to be in politics twenty-four hours a day. He knew that prolonged tension and uncontrollable fear can always reach a point where the loyalty of men to their party or to their nation gives out, and where the most rudimentary elements of individual self-respect and decency vanish. Because men have nerves, a situation can always be created, a point can always be reached, where man can be unnerved.

Hitler did not originate these conditions of tension and corruption. He did not even create fascism. An amateur evil-doer, Mussolini, had already stumbled into the discovery of fascism. Hitler took all the elements of corruption and decay inherent in our society and made of them fascism—a bundle of forces tied together to give evil in our time its most hard-hitting edge.

There have been other men, other so-called leaders of fascism, who have made deliberate use of this evil to satisfy their vanity or their greed. Hitler wished for evil with total ascetic dedication. He never wanted anything but evil, and his measure of evil was always total evil. He followed the same techniques undeviatingly against internal and external enemies in war and in peace. In fact, he never made any distinction between war and peace. He looked upon the leaders of other nations as social democrats to be cowed or plutocrats to be duped. The boundary line between politics and economics, government and business, he found as easy to violate as that between domestic and external politics. He used and exploded the principle of self-determination in order to conquer Europe, just as he had used and exploded the civil liberties of the Weimar Republic in order to conquer power.

The last thing that Hitler used and exploded was his

own fascism. He drove fascism to its ultimate extreme, showed it as an element of destruction for all nations, just as he had driven all the main conflicts and contradictions of our society to their final spasm.

In no case, under no circumstances, could he ever have won. Every time he neared final victory he found it blocked by a triumph he had already achieved. His bloodless conquests were stopped by Munich because exasperated men everywhere decided that anything was better than a new Munich. The work of traitors in countries marked for invasion became very difficult after internal treason acquired the name of Quisling. Collaboration in a country that Hitler had defeated was unmistakably defined by the face of Laval. A few quislings in some countries barred the way to more quislings in other countries. One after another, he exhausted all his weapons: first blackmail, then treason, then a mixture of violence and treason. When he attacked Russia the weapon of sheer violence failed him. It seemed for a while as if the world could not stand his threat of total war. Then the fliers of Great Britain and the soldiers of Russia proved that they could take Hitler's total war and fight it back. From then on his mad fury began to spend itself.

It has been the tragedy of the United Nations to have to fight an enemy who could not win and with whom they could make no peace. This fact freed Hitler from all restraint and allowed him to bring into the world the fullest measure of destruction that was at his command. The last we saw of him was an unreal image of furious helplessness. As a man he was the concentration of all evil, but the war itself went far beyond him, reached proportions, acquired a scope and a depth, that he could neither control nor measure. In fact, Hitler and his ilk were not the makers but the remorseless parasites of disaster.

He was merely an agent of destruction, not the cause of it. He did not bring about the intensification of political warfare in our world, the technique of the war of nerves, the machinations of quislings, or the existence of international political parties. Most of the institutions he destroyed, the conventions of domestic and international politics he exploded, were ready for destruction and explosion. Many of the doors he broke through were unlocked or unhinged. He was the only one who derived no advantage from so much wrecking, because he never cared for advantage but only for wrecking.

In our postwar world, democracy and communism pursue their conflict with the technique of the war of nerves, as a preventive and a substitute for armed warfare. The boundary lines between domestic and external politics in every nation that Hitler crushed have not been rebuilt. Rather, for every country in Europe and Asia, the chances of survival and stable national order depend largely on the international policies of the major powers.

The world we live in is the world Hitler left us. Each single element that was wrong with our world has been high-lighted by the flames of his destruction. We are now moving along the ground that he laid waste—and that he opened up. We take advantage of techniques he was the first to use. The major powers are now waging political warfare against each other, and will go on waging it for a long time. They will intervene in the domestic affairs of the minor nations all over the world, under cover of the principle of non-interference and the doctrine of self-determination, now quoted from their latest text, the United Nations Charter.

The end of the war and Hitler's disappearance have at the same time revived the ceremonial of verbal respect for old principles and strengthened the forces which tend to obliterate them. Democracy and communism, each strengthened by its contribution to the common victory, are still as opposed to each other and suspicious of each other as at the time when fascism, the self-appointed arbiter, the third force of the time, cut short their struggle and humiliated both. Actually, both democracy and communism had been defeated in every round they fought with fascism up to the time that fascism itself brought war to them. Each found a way to counteract fascism in wartime, after having failed to find a way in peacetime.

Hitler's path to victory was blocked by every one of his triumphs until, at the end, his last hope of victory was to create by his disappearance a condition of things where the uncontrolled strife of democracy and communism might again work for him.

He must not succeed, in fact, it is up to us, his non-communist enemies, to see that he does not succeed and that his death may prove final. For he has left us much wiser than we were: we have learned to give the lie to the alleged landslides of history, to the fraudulent portents of irreversible destiny. We know now what the elements are that weaken or threaten our civilization, and that must be taken care of, if communist aggressiveness is to be stopped. And now we have a name, Hitler, for that third solution which pretends to cut short the conflict between democracy and communism. We cannot run away from ourselves, we cannot become the frenzied image of our opponent. On all sides, Hitler has marked the ways that are barred to us.

That is why we cannot let him go. People all over the world have a right to know what can be done to prevent a recurrence of that blight. They have a right to ask what it was in their institutions that left them so exposed. And they must be answered clearly and definitely with institutions that work and principles that give light.

CHAPTER III

BETWEEN WAR AND PEACE

From the beginning it was a baffling war, and this is a baffling peace. When war finally came it was so different from what we had expected that in the first few months we called it "phony." There was a phony, unreal quality about peace too, when at long last war ended. Or perhaps it was our way of coping with both war and peace when they came that was unreal and phony.

Never was a war so fully expected and foreseen in dread and fear by such large masses of people. Never was peace so desperately coveted by so many millions of men and women who had gone far beyond the ultimate stretch of what human nature can endure. But when, in their own way and time, war and peace came, the people realized that they had no preparation for them and no adequate name.

This curse of misnaming things and misdirecting efforts has been with us for a long time. In the case of the United States, every single step designed to keep the country out of war, or to limit its contribution to it, turned out to be a step toward war. England was brought into the war by way of Munich, and Soviet Russia by the pact of '39;

while the enemy was driven into war because it stretched too far its impudent abuse of peace.

Before the war, peace was not peace, and now, after the war, there is victory but not peace. Something has gone wrong in the relationship between what we do and what we think we do, our efforts and our reckoning of them, our idea of things and our experience with them.

This was no ordinary war. It made feverish and inadequate our organs of perception and reasoning, and it came because our organs of political intelligence and political action were feverish and inadequate.

All along, this has been the world civil war. The fundamental relationships of men are radically upset all over the world—men and their ideas, men and their instruments of production.

It was a war of all the people, but it started everywhere with the least possible degree of popular enthusiasm; it was called a war of ideas, but it was fought with the least possible display of ideas.

There have not been many songs born of this war in any country. The songwriters were busy, as were the manipulators of propaganda slogans. But warlike tunes and stirring battle cries bore too embarrassing a resemblance to those of the last war. It was as if our best emotional ammunition had been shot a quarter of a century ago. It was hard to say, even if anyone felt it, that this was a war to end war and to make the world safe for democracy. The memory of the last time clogged with self-consciousness the expression of our beliefs.

The enemy peoples had lived for years in a condition

of war, training for war, and when the fighting actually started they were like an army shifted from one front to another. On our side, the people tackled this war as a hard job to be done. This businesslike attitude led to a strong emphasis on the role of technique and skill.

In America we mobilized along the lines of crafts and skills. The implication seemed to be that as far as possible every soldier should be channeled into the kind of work he had done in civilian life, and that the army could train unskilled workers for specialized jobs. The distinction between the army and the nation, the discipline of war and the discipline of peace, was sharply reduced. Increasingly, the way in which men pay their obligation of citizenship in wartime is determined by the kind of tools they have learned to handle.

Among the various skills we mobilized were those of the propaganda specialist, the public relations counsel, the expert on the rights of men. It was said from the start that we needed war aims and peace aims. But the awareness of this need far preceded any tentative formulation. We wanted to believe in something when we did not know what to believe; and this made the formulation of our beliefs, when we arrived at it, vague and rhetorical.

From start to finish, it was a very queer war. It reached every man, every type and class and nation of men, in a kaleidoscopic variety of ways, showing different facets to different people on different occasions. It was a war filled with more horrors than the human mind could grasp, yet for long stretches of time it came to be accepted by practically everybody as an inescapable part of the business of living. It was in actuality one war fought in one world, in the sense that it engulfed all men and on its outcome their future depended. Yet for all its oneness it was a strange collection of many different wars.

At first it showed itself in samples. A single nation, as in the case of Poland, Finland and Norway, was crushed by a superior enemy who wanted to test his might and at the same time intimidate all the other nations. Lightning violence was added to the armory of the war of nerves. It was used surgically in the most neuralgic spots where the greatest advantage could be gained by a realistic display of ruthlessness. That was the strange time of the phony war. People everywhere—not only in America—could choose their war among the several available. The propertied classes were for Finland, intellectuals and socialites for France, while the upper middle classes collected bundles for Britain and a few groups of missionaries fixed their eyes on China. Some unorthodox intellectuals and left-wing liberals found none of these sample wars to their taste, since they were still nostalgic for the war in Spain.

Then the picture changed, and the politically minded groups were tossed around. Some pro-French socialites turned from enmity to a benevolent reserve toward Hitler, while shortly afterwards the communists all over the world went from radical pacifism to the most belligerent hatred of nazism.

This war of one world was scattered in a number of private wars actually fought or merely threatened. There was the war of Russia against Finland and of Finland against Russia. In France there was the exploitation of defeat for purposes of civil war, and in Asia there was, and still is, the irrepressible struggle of the native peoples against European rule. The partisan armies fighting fascists in Yugoslavia and Greece fought their own civil war on the side.

We had to recognize it as one war fought in one world because unmistakable facts made it so. But our understanding was always trotting belatedly behind the facts, and to be convinced that these facts were part of one pattern—one war in one world—we needed the help of a map and the reports of world-girdling travelers. Yet we had to cling to this conviction every time we had to reconcile ourselves to the strange alliance that the chances of war—and the will of Hitler—had imposed on us.

It was an all-consuming war. It consumed the men who were responsible for it and the peoples from which they sprang, just as it consumed the reservoirs of physical and moral resources on the winning side.

Mussolini, hailed and cursed as a great arsonist, is now an embarrassing memory to friends and enemies alike, so inept and grotesque did he prove when burned by real fire. Hitler appeared insecure and unreal the moment victory seemed within his reach. These two rode the crest of the surging wave and acted as if it were they who ruled its course. Dogs may bark at the rising moon, but it is not their barking that makes the moon rise.

The German state vanished, and in its stead was left the German people, wards of the Allies. In demanding the unconditional surrender of Germany, the Allies acknowledged a pattern that nazism itself had created; there was no one in Germany with authority or dignity enough to accept or obey any conditions. The Allies had no choice: they had to impose an unconditional surrender or else reenthrone fascism. The unconditional surrender of Germany was a direct result of the unconditional obedience that nazism had extorted from the German people.

Our nations too have undergone a process of consumption, each of them remaining what it used to be, only less so: England less of an empire, the United States and Russia less isolated in their proud independence of the rest of the world, and all the other nations on our side incomparably shrunken.

It was a war of denials. What will perhaps most stir the imagination of our children will be the memory of a gigantic "no": the "no" of a united China after the fall of Canton in 1938; of Churchill's England in the summer and fall of 1940; of De Gaulle's France refusing to acknowledge defeat; of Stalin's Russia during two summers. It will be forever true that these no's changed the course of history. Yet the no's which all the people on our side flung in the face of Hitler and his order were so costly and exacting that they left little energy to be spent in positive assertions.

The fighting ended as it had begun, in a scattered, fitful way. The moments of victory were spread over too many days of postponed announcements to be celebrated with the outbursts of joy that the hearts of millions had been anticipating for so long. There was no decisiveness in the event and no relief from crushing worries, because there was still no peace.

Within the span of a few weeks, when the military struggle was in its final phase, the two most impudent mouthpieces of evil vanished. Concurrently, Churchill was forced out of his country's government and Roosevelt died. The era of men who in lieu of ideas had given a positive or negative direction to the conflict was over.

Greatness of soul, of vision and courage, represented above all others by Roosevelt, came close to the point of finishing the job and stopped there. The whole of civilized mankind had learned to recognize its hopes in Roosevelt's person. The shock of his death fell upon utterly worn-out men and women who could do nothing but bow their heads and weep for the death of a man who had been their best friend. Never was a great man so honored as Roosevelt, because never did a statesman succeed as Roosevelt did in becoming a friend of the human race.

With the man gone whose presence had replaced ideas, peace appeared bitterly phony and the world a dismal sight. A civil war, world-wide in scope, had preceded the shooting war. The shooting war was, in fact, only an accidental phase of the world civil war. When the shooting ended, the process started moving at a slower tempo which was called peace.

This is a very peculiar civil war. It is civil because it affects the very substance of the relationship between the citizen and his community. It is world-wide because no nation is exempt from its disturbance. Its essence lies in the fact that most of the tools created by human ingenuity have gotten, in varying degree, out of hand. They may be weapons devised by science, like those of modern technology, dramatized now by the atom bomb; or they may be weapons perfected by centuries of political experience, like the modern state and international political parties, dramatized now by international communism, Russia's counterpart of the atom bomb.

The ideas upon which civilization stands have gone underground. We do not refer to them, except in a dry, catechistic way or for Fourth of July celebration. Actually, this last phase of the world civil war is marked by the absence of beliefs more than by their conflict.

A democracy, devitalized by the unthinking reiteration of its principles, is facing communism that is becoming increasingly the diligent collection of the most contradictory commonplaces of the last hundred years—from the unrestrained sovereignty of nations to the unrelieved subjection of men to economic forces. Each of the conflicting ideologies advocated as universally valid a type of organization of labor and a mode of living which actually is only remotely approximated by the nation that champions it. Both ideologies have become stale, since for the better part of a century there has been no attempt to check their postulates and aims against the facts of modern life. Everywhere in the world people are drawn to one side or the other and tossed from one side to the other, for reasons that have less and less to do with allegiance to an ideal. The fury of the battle grows in direct proportion to its ideological confusion.

Yet there is a groping mending process creeping in our world, as if the moral and physical effort that brought victory in the war had counteracted the slumber of ideas. Somehow, we do things, we take initiatives that contradict the still widespread sense of hopelessness and doom. Sometimes, our groping actions appear to be wiser than our wisdom. Somewhere, we succeed in putting brakes to forces that seemed to be beyond our control. In this country, after having gone through a process of mad and almost suicidal demobilization, after having with unconscionable abruptness cut the economic assistance to our democratic allies, finally with the Marshall Plan we have given help and hope to the world. We find in the continental grouping of states a device that may allow the weaker nations to hold together, so that their pooled or co-ordinated resources may be adequate to their needs.

It is a slow, yet unmistakable process. It has become clear now that the democratic powers, above all the United States, must in their own interest sustain the weaker nations on their road to independence and self-reliance. The interest of the United States is to have self-supporting partners and not parasitical satellites, and to create conditions of national or continental independence that might check the recklessness of the major powers—including the United States. Pursuit of this policy hampers the tortuous course of the non-democratic nations, increasingly forced to rely on patterns and traditions that too few years ago were violently exposed by Hitler.

We know the chain reaction that from the decay of democracy led to communism and from the struggle between communism and democracy led to Hitler. Once Hitler was gone, the world had to face the conditions that made Hitler possible, and so it was proper that democracy had once more to face the communist attack. For Stalin is not Hitler, but one of the main causes which led to Hitler. The other main cause lies inside democracy.

Thus, by slowly grappling with the chain of causes, from the most immediate and compelling to the most remote and fundamental, men will bring under control the forces preying on them. The victory over fascism proves that more than half of the job is done.

Slowly and gropingly, the effort is being made to uncover the major causes of disturbance and to tackle them one by one. There are new ties being established among nations and parties, cutting across national traditions and national boundaries, mitigating both the dependence of the weak nations and the power of the great ones. There are things happening in the world of power politics that go vastly beyond our experience with politics or with power.

The mending process goes on for the most part unnoticed and unsung, often with the appearance or the threat of disaster. It goes on in fragments, in a scattered tumultuous way, just as the war did. But now, in the political phase of the world civil war, we can learn to recognize the character and the direction of the forces that are making or un-making our world. Now we can again have aims and seek the right proportion between goals and means, things and their names.

CHAPTER IV

WE, THE PEOPLE

THE world civil war was accompanied by the most deafening ideological warfare, but throughout its military phase it became a mute war. There was a moratorium on ideologies in the world.

Before the first World War and during most of the nineteenth century, visionaries and ideologists were continually propounding radically new departures in political living. The air was filled with talk of revolution. Yet in all that time there was not a revolution of any importance in the Western world. It was as if unparalleled economic creativeness had numbed political thinking.

Then between the two wars all the ideologies that had been vocally and harmlessly advocated had their chance to be tried out. In our day communism is no longer the esoteric and seditious program of a few international outlaws who derived their inspiration from an abstruse book. The theory of racial purity, culled from the glittering generalities of a handful of international snobs, came down to earth in articles and paragraphs of law ruthlessly enforced, which prescribed the wholesale slaughtering of men, women and children. The Christian democracy of the papal encyclicals was for a time the law of Dollfus' Austria. Social democracy, too, had its chance in the Germany of Weimar and in Republican Spain. Even Charles Maurras' national revolution was tested in the dishonored France of Vichy.

The people had no protection against the raids of promoters of new ways of living. The acid of ideas permeated them, corroded and burned them. In nearly every nation of Europe the people were given in holocaust to some ideological god.

After so much talking by the few, so much suffering by the many, a saturation point has been reached, marked by the amount of suffering that men can bear. There are definite limits to the game of power politics, both national and international, limits which are determined by the human substance on which the game is played. There is a limit both to what men can take and to what can be taken out of men. Some small latter-day Machiavellis think that the institutions which govern the lives of men rest simply on the shrewdness or ruthlessness of political operators. They think the sky is the limit to the experiments that can be tried out on human flesh.

We talk of our institutions of government as symbols, of our beliefs as myths. Somehow, we forget that the symbols actually symbolize the interests, the feelings, the very lives of the people, and that myths are patterns of behavior and of beliefs that men live by. We think there is no other limit to the tailoring of new institutions than the skill with which the cutting is devised. But the stuff which is cut into is man's life.

We talk about nations and classes and cultures and civilizations. These figures of speech are our tools, the instruments we use to visualize a complex world and to exert

some control over it. But the people are the reality of what
is a figure of our speech.

"The people" is not a rhetorical name for the generality
of human beings living in a certain commonwealth. Neither
is it a name for skimmed mankind. The people is all of us—,
doing our jobs according to the training we have had, the
luck we enjoy, the group to which we happen to belong.
The individual who holds power, no matter how great, is
a particle of the people, acting for them because he is one
of them, and taking chances far beyond his own capacity
to pay. The power he wields, be it that of money or of
politics or of expression, does not belong to him. Whether
it be self-assumed or granted by democratic procedure,
when those who handle it fail, the people pay.

Nor is there much meaning in the use of the word
"common" when prefixed to the word "people." Perhaps
we should say humble—provided we understand that
humility, which is a condition for the many, is a duty for
the few who, by virtue of their gifts or their luck, assume
the privilege of acting for the many.

The appeal to the "common people" is bad demagoguery
if it implies that the populace, the larges masses of citizens
of any given commonwealth, are at all times aware of their
purposes and interests and have, each one of them or all
of them as a whole, the same skill in judgment and action
as must be mastered by those to whom they have entrusted
power.

When the people are flattered by attributions of omnip-
otence and omniscience, the responsibility of those who
hold their power in trust is reduced. The more the "com-

mon" is flattered, the more hopelessly he is at the mercy of the "uncommon." It is a hard discipline for people to acquire, that of listening to themselves and checking the voice of their spokesmen, so as to find out their own will and carry it through. This discipline is called democracy.

The people express themselves through instruments of recognition and representation. In themselves these instruments, no matter what the political order may be, are mere legalistic gadgets. Of themselves all representatives, no matter whether they are the people's choice or anointed kings, are little more than puppets. For the people are the absolute reality of what is played and represented on the political stage. But if we consider the organs of recognition and representation as alien to or superimposed upon this complex reality that is called the people, then we reduce the people to a rabble. For this debasement, the people pay.

The fiduciary nature of the political and social order, the fact that the people always pay in the end, never remains hidden for long. Occasions always come when the symbols of government have to be buttressed by the physical support of those who are symbolized by them, or when the circulation of political notes has to be backed by the citizens' blood. Moments always come when the commitments of the few have to be met by drawing upon the sweat and tears of the many.

If the response to "idealism" has been half-hearted during the last phases of the world civil war, this does not mean that the people have reverted to a brutish or "materialistic" temper, forcing upon the professional manipulators of ideas a sort of seasonal unemployment. It is rather that there has been too much stirring of human hopes—too much of it for too long a time, and at too heavy a price. Hitler came at the end of a long, long series of melodramatic interpretations of history, spirited calls to destiny, sickening displays of Machiavellian ruthlessness. Hitler's was the last epileptic spasm of the old "idealism," the most reckless of the ideologies babbling itself into mania.

The birth of the United Nations has hardly been accompanied by any great display of ideological inventiveness. In fact, many people have shied away from the UN for its too striking resemblance to the League of Nations. The name United Nations came before the notion of what it was supposed to mean and long before the organs capable of making it a workable institution. As for the idea itself, it is still hazy.

The UN was not born at San Francisco or Dumbarton Oaks. It grew out of the hushed discussions of the Chancelleries; and whenever it became an object of public debate in formal international conferences its growth appeared seriously endangered. The Charter starts with the words "We, the Peoples. . . ." Yet nowhere have the peoples been consulted as to the main principles for which the organization is to stand.

The "We" seems so far to mean the quarrelsome, verbose representatives of the peoples, many of whom have a rather doubtful claim to their representative capacity. On the floodlighted stage of the United Nations the actors frequently seem to be overacting. Yet it is on this stage that the gaze of the peoples of the world is riveted. They see the inadequate actors, hear the sometimes sickening eloquence. Though they rarely applaud or hiss, their eyes remain fixed on that platform where the shortcomings of

our leaders and institutions so powerfully denounce themselves. The performance, far from being reassuring, keeps
the world jittery. But it is this constant scrutiny that
keeps the show from falling apart.

The people are tired of being misled or unled, of being
flattered by the attribution of fullness of power and wisdom, or deprived of even the narrowest margin of personal independence. They do not lose sight of the UN
because the organization summarizes and makes visible on
a world-wide scale the elements that hamper the coming
of peace. And above all, it is peace they want. After the
payments exacted by the war to redeem the pledges of
politicians and theorists, mankind is not inclined to destroy
itself for the sake of verifying theories and confirming
predictions.

Everywhere, the relationship has been upset between
the people and their institutions, between the citizens and
those who hold in trust their economic, intellectual or
political power. When institutions too frequently demand
that the fiduciary circulation of their policies be redeemed
by the citizens' lives, it is obvious that such institutions do
not work. When ideologies are paid for in terms of constantly disrupted peace, and the arrogance of theories
makes impossible a quiet, humble existence for the many,
then the ideologies and theories, too, are of no use.

For public exercise of intelligence, as of any other type
of power, is the administration of other people's destinies.
It is not an art or profession to be cultivated for mere
profit or mere fun. It carries accountabilities proportionate
to the influence it exerts.

The people everywhere cannot afford any longer the
nervous disorders and the intellectual recklessness of the
men who are supposed to lead them or to think for them.

Perhaps the silence of ideologists during the last war is not to be entirely deplored; perhaps it was the best thing we could do to fight a mute war. Perhaps the fact that the ideas upon which civilization is rooted have gone underground means that there they have a chance to grow.

AMERICA

THIS civil war that exploded at the end of the first World War was in the making for a long time—ever since national states were established in Europe; in fact ever since America was discovered. Its causes may have been befogged, its omens misinterpreted by writers and statesmen, but harassed people in every country of Europe somehow had known all along that they were being trapped, and they looked for a way out. The more convulsive life became on the old continent, the more numerous were the men who, as if driven by the instinct of the race, looked for lands where they might have a chance to work in peace. America, North and South, was the place where men went who wanted to be free from hopelessness.

The so-called isolationism of the American people has considerably deeper foundations than the Declaration of Independence and Washington's Farewell Address. Every immigrant who uprooted himself from his native country and settled here celebrated his independence from the destiny of Europe. This went on for three centuries. As fascism was the convergence of all the hopelessness of Europe, so the very existence of America was the repudiation of it. But this repudiation had already been made once by every man and woman who came to live here, and when the Old World was being consumed every American in his bones knew why.

When the second World War started, if Americans did not know exactly what they loved, they certainly knew what they hated. They hated Hitler. It was in them to hate Hitler. He had made them uncomfortable even when he followed policies that one or another of their own groups had already advocated—policies like the curbing of trade unions, or the control of capitalism, or anti-Semitism, or the unification of Europe. They hated him because they feared him. They hated and feared him when he appeared similar to some of them, and they hated and feared him when he showed himself to be thoroughly different from them. They hated him because at all possible costs they did not want to be like him—or like his victims.

They knew that what was happening in Europe was the result of a long, long series of mistakes and crimes, that the nations of Europe should have found some way to get along and live together in tolerance, just as in America men of all races—no angels, no better than their relatives in Europe—had managed to form a new, fairly united community.

From the very beginning this time, the stakes appeared terribly high and the betting unusually risky. The time before, it had taken the American people three years to move from the spectators' seats into the arena. They had gone into the fight to put a stop to it; and they were so certain that their intervention would determine the coming of peace that they laid down fourteen points on which the peace was to be founded.

This time it was different. There was never any doubt

about which side the American people favored. There was very little room for propaganda or announcements of intention or clever exchanges of diplomatic papers. Through their radio and their press the American people, from Munich on, had themselves been present. They looked at things for themselves, and things had an appalling clarity. Hitler was branding the people of Europe like cattle; he was deliberately attempting to mold Europe into exactly the opposite of what America was meant to be.

The realization gradually dawned in the minds of an increasing number of Americans that Hitler was after them. And in very fact he was after them, whether he planned it so or not. Even if he never mentioned them, the American people and their way of life were his ultimate target. It was obvious that if Hitler was out to re-introduce slavery into the world, he would be bound to bring the American people back to the condition of hopelessness from which they or their fathers had long ago escaped. He was bound to make Europeans again of all of them.

Still, Hitler was far away, and a long time passed between the first lightning on the horizon and the first bolt on American soil. In the hearts of the American people there was a feeling of unreality, a sickening apprehension that marred all reasoned judgment. It was as if they could never succeed in convincing themselves of the truth of what they saw or the soundness of what they felt.

Even after Pearl Harbor there remained a feeling of unreality about this war, as if the people had been stunned more than convinced. War was brought home to them when the production of things designed to make life comfortable, to spread and maintain their standard of living, suddenly stopped. Everything that their industry had been manufacturing appeared then to have been merely a rehearsal, a trial sample of what American technology and manpower could do.

America has been called the arsenal of democracy. In its participation in the war, it revealed itself as much more than that. For three hundred years, as if the instinct of the race had been looking for a safe cache, the skills and traditions of civilization, the outpouring of all the races of Europe, had been stored here. It was difficult until then to know what this meant in the universal order of things. America was neither a colony, nor an annex, nor a caricature of Europe. Enormous, fleshy, and somehow shapeless, it was an easy target for the irony of visitors from the old continent, a picture of the future that possibly was in store for all men but that was hardly alluring to many of them.

With every shipment of Lend-Lease material that left this continent during the war, it became more apparent that this was no appendage of Europe that had been organized here, no oddity of Europe marginal to the old continent, but a great storehouse of the hopes and skills of men, on which all Western civilization could draw.

Americans had created an enormous wealth and lavishly played with it. They had enjoyed the settling of open spaces, the extending of continental highways, as a sort of holiday from scarcity imposed on men by a nature that long exploitation had made stingy. It was, as well, a holiday from the responsibilities imposed by superior wealth and power.

There was something casual and experimental in the way America had been organized: a rapid passing from infancy to decay, as evidenced by almost every American city; a recurrent restlessness, an urge to move on that set new wheels rolling on the old wagon trails.

The war opened the storehouse for universal use. The fact that the goal of American production had been the manufacture of articles intended to make life comfortable and pleasant did not mean that the American people had gone soft. The fact that industrial production had been rapidly converted to the manufacture of war materials did not mean that the American people had gone into the business of killing and destroying. It was the volume and speed of production that were more important than any of its immediate objectives.

America is an experiment conducted and developed over the course of three centuries, an experiment of a section of mankind that succeeded in organizing itself by bringing together, in the full light of history and publicity, men of most of the races of the world. It is by no means a concluded or a thoroughly successful experiment. Its achievements are marred by shocking, well-publicized yet still uncorrected contradictions. The experiment has been carried on in exceptional and scarcely repeatable circumstances, somewhat on the margin of European and world history, thanks to a private continental condition of peace that two oceans seemed to guarantee.

For all its blundering, for all its feverish improvisation and occasional cruelty, the American experiment has fostered the growth of a type of man strong in his muscles, humorous, realistic and kind; a type of man that is still to a large extent in the making but that has exhibited conclusive evidence of what the human race can do if only it can enjoy peace and devote itself to work.

This storehouse of civilization does not offer a political

and social pattern for universal imitation and adoption. But it does offer a frame of mind, a type of man, an immeasurable reservoir of ingenuity and labor.

Actually, the war was a war of liberation for the American people no less than for the people of Europe. For Americans it was liberation from the danger of succumbing to the destiny of Europe and of losing their independence from Europe. It was liberation from an old tendency to become ingrown, to live a private history as a superfluous nation dedicated to the production of the comfortable superfluities of life.

If the American experiment were a concluded and perfected experiment, if it furnished a pattern of political and social organization to be adopted by or imposed on every people on earth, then the war would have turned into one of imperial conquest by the American people. As it is, it offers enough experience to fall back on, just as it afforded enough power to win the war; but neither its power nor its experience is sufficient to make dispensable the cooperation of all men.

As soon as the "Cease Fire" sounded on the distant fronts of Europe and Asia, the American people thought they would have peace. They rushed into peace, tearing away restrictions, clamoring to have back the unhampered possession of their highways and machines and gadgets, of all the things that make American life abundant. Just as the sudden loss of these things had meant that the job of war was beginning, so the end of the job of war seemed to mean that peace was back to be enjoyed. In the orgy of demobilization and reconversion, there was triumphant confidence that the American experiment could resume its private course.

When the war in Europe started, the American people, although they hated Hitler, could not quite decide if and when and how they had to fight Hitler. When hostilities ended, they could not quite decide what to make of the power that victory had put in their hands. There was, however, one fact they had to face. At the end of the war the American people found that all over the world were men who believed in them and what they stood for, that in every country in the world there were partisans of America. The American government found that it had a much larger constituency than the American citizenry.

This is an unprecedented situation, as was unprecedented the fact of a great people emerging victorious from a horrible war, seeking exoneration from world leadership. At the end of the first World War America succeeded in rejecting the responsibility of its power by repudiating the League of Nations. At the end of the second World War America tried to reach the same goal by entrusting the victory she had conquered to the machinery of the United Nations. Yet there was no escape, no exemption on any ground—even that of unfitness. There was no immunity to be had through nationalism or through internationalism, because of humility or because of pride. However reluctantly, America is a partisan leader in the world civil war.

These sons of immigrants from all over the world form one of the least worldly and least cosmopolitan of the great nations. But now and forever America has lost its isolation—that sometimes odd, sometimes glorious peculiarity of being the only great nation on earth founded on a mode of living. America used to be the only self-started nation that owed its existence to a revolution and its

development to the unrestrained adoption of industrialism.
In the Soviet Union it has found its match.

Within the United Nations and on every single political
battleground in the world America has to compete with
another nation that like herself embodies a mode of life.
This competition is of universal scope and is susceptible
to measurement at every point. It cannot be resolved
simply by establishing zones of influence. It is the conflict
of two different systems for regulating the relationship
between men and their means of production and is actually
or potentially fought in every workshop. There is no purpose in beclouding the results of the two systems by
theoretical discussion, since they can be gauged by the
standard of living and the happiness of the peoples who
have adopted them.

Competition has always been an American ideal and one
of the secrets of American creativeness. The only thing
for which there was no competition was America itself.
Before the world civil war, America had been an isolated
experiment, awe-inspiring, oversized and somehow incongruous. Now in order to win the world civil war, it
must justify itself, its principles and its results. It must
bring satisfaction to its own people in order to keep their
loyalty and the respect of the world. Because it now has
a competitor, it must increasingly become what it was always supposed to be: the exemplary organization of a
mode of life, the focus from which men of all nations can
draw orientation and strength. The great danger for
America was always that of turning into a nation like any

other nation or into an empire. Now it is the focal point
of an internationale.

During a century and a half, men have developed here
a blend of machine-age democracy and of the old European tradition of rights and freedom under law. It is not
a blend that can be adopted everywhere by an easy process
of imitation. But its high degree of tested success, the
large experience that men have acquired in applying it to
various contingencies, give us the only reservoir of experience on which we can draw in order to know how to
proceed in rebuilding a world where the traditions and
institutions of freedom have been shaken to their foundations. Here we have the only pattern of a civilization built
not on a sheer interpretation of economic forces, but on a
constant reciprocal adjustment betwen those forces and
the institutions of freedom.

The nation least inclined to be swept by ideological
recklessness is challenged by another nation driven by the
most uncompromising ideological dogmatism. America
cannot answer any longer that her principles and her per-
formances are nobody else's concern, without at the same
time declaring her own bankruptcy. The civil war will
end when men are freed from the fear of being swept away
by their instruments of production and of government.
America is the only nation vigorous enough to bring to an
end the civil war, by re-establishing in the societies of men
the power to check the drifts of economics, of politics and
of ideologies.

The war has destroyed institutions, cultures and wealths
far beyond our capacity to measure. At the same time it
has revealed the existence of some formidable irreducible
realities. The people have never appeared so unmistakably
as the absolute reality on which all our institutions of

politics and economics are founded. America was never so real as when she was fighting the war under Roosevelt. The present political phase of the war offers America a role at least as great.

Today the principles of American life have become the belief and hope of the partisans of America all over the world. Should these partisans be crushed by communism, the principles of American life would not be safe even on American soil. Should the conflict with Russia develop into military war, fascism might take over. This is in the nature of things, here and everywhere. The time seems to have come when the concept of freedom for which America stands must be restated in all its aggressiveness as the necessary weapon for the political struggle in which we are engaged.

PART II

FREEDOM

CHAPTER I

WHAT MAKES FREEDOM

T HE EXPERIENCE of freedom is so closely bound up with the experience of work that no one can know freedom unless he knows how to work. Work is the common substance from which derive all the various types of freedom that the individual or the community may enjoy. The raw material that our social organs process into political, religious or intellectual freedom is produced at the cost of our sweat and toil.

We are made by what we do. The obstacles we have to master, the efforts we have to sustain, give us a measure of our power. We subject our moods to the discipline of our work and our work to the discipline we have imposed on ourselves.

At the end of a task or at the end of a day we take leave from what we have done and revert to ourselves. We look back at what has been our effort, we compare what we expected with what has happened, we reckon what we intended to do with what we actually did. What we do is always done with others and for others; but when our effort is still a fresh recollection, bringing us a measure of our power, then the work we have done really becomes our own.

The builders of the Pyramids were not made free by their work, and the forced laborers in the Siberian camps are every day more enslaved by what they have to do. So it is not our work that makes us free but our possibility of returning from our work to ourselves. Freedom is the name for a particular mode of producing and using the power that man releases.

Freedom is a mode of labor that allows the worker to recover the energy he has spent—to recover it with a personal profit. It is net income from work well done.

We are made by what we do. Yet we know that our work is well done only when we find in it evidence that we can do more and better work, that what has been the object of hard exertion can be looked at as just a sample.

We are made, but we can also be unmade, by what we do. What we do can make or unmake us according to our capacity for recapturing the energy we have invested in our work and for bringing back to our work the skill we have derived from it. This is the dynamo that converts labor into freedom and laborers into men.

The artist and the artisan know this when they bring all their skill to bear on the object of their work and make of it something that is finished, concluded, well done— something that is made by an individual person but carries a collective meaning. The essential purpose and the essential meaning is the constant growth, the constant enrichment of freedom that becomes intensely communicative and aggressive when much skillful and purposeful power is molded in some piece of material—a fragment of marble or wood or steel, a sequence of words, or a series of musical sounds. The farmer knows something of freedom when he harvests his crop after a year's struggle with the hazards of weather. Every workman gets a glimpse of freedom when, at the end of his day, he feels in his tired bones the energy he has spent and tries to figure out what his lot is and how it can be improved.

Men can be wasteful and awkward in handling their freedom, just as they can be wasteful of all their other products. They seldom know how to use it when they have it, or how to think of it when they are slaves. When they are slaves they dream of freedom as a divine remedy that will cure all their ills, and when they have some part of freedom they are likely to squander it because they fail to recognize that it is man-made, specific and limited.

Our civilization was made possible because men learned how to recapture the energy they had invested in their work, to make experience of it, to acquire a better control over the conditions of their labor and do a better job. Men gain freedom as a by-product of their labor and find in it the chance to make of their labor a by-product of their power. Civilization began when men discovered that there is a fissionable quality in their labor and that by controlling the fission of freedom from labor they could exert a measure of control over their own lives.

There can be no freedom unless there is obedience and exertion, unless there is independence and recovery of energy. The obedience is always to something specific and measurable, something that our forces can cope with; the independence as specific and defined as the exertion has been.

Nor can men ever be free simply for the sake or the fun of being free, squandering in personal enjoyment the individual returns they have earned. Their freedom must be freedom to do something, freedom from something, for the purpose of attaining something. Bit by bit, in small groups or large, with losses and reverses and blunders, men gain freedom *from* some of the conditions of their life, *to* strengthen their own power in relation to certain definite things, *for* reducing some of the obstacles that stand in their way.

Freedom is power, a concentrated, skillful capacity to act. It is a constant high-tension release of energy, and not a state of bliss. It is not the privilege of the unborn or the dead, but the spark that evinces the living. Never vague, it is always embodied in the worker or in the object of his work. Whether residing in the object of exertion or filtered, refurbished in the individual, whether subject to the discipline of obedience or making for independence, this mode of labor, of man-made and man-making power, is always purposeful and specific.

It is the function of freedom to make a dent in the sullenness of man's nature. It is the hard-won privilege of hard-working men, of men who are limited in their power but ready to take chances, to mix with other men, to get muddy and dirty—of men who know how to set themselves a goal and to retrace their course so as to make order out of the tumult from which they have emerged. Civilization has been made by people who wormed their way through the resistance of physical or human nature and who of the secrets they conquered made the experience of the race.

We live and work in swarms as the bees do. We gain our lives in the society of our fellow beings because there is no work that is not done in society and for society. But only the individual can make and know freedom. The life of a man who does his work well is marked by a double process like the pulsation of the human heart: the outgoing of his exertion, the intaking of his experience. There is no intake unless there is outgo, and what we take in is always the experience of our exertion. Yet when we weave the loose threads of our doings into the texture of our individual person, then we do not lift ourselves above society but bring our fullest contribution to it. The protagonist of freedom is the individual, but its production is always a social venture. This dynamism makes workers into men, masses or herds into societies.

If we are able to communicate with one another and exchange the products of our labor, if what we do and experience has meaning and value to others, this is due only to the fact that the experience we gain out of our labor is fundamentally the same for all. The freedom that has been produced and stored in the world since civilization began is the primary value, the basic coin immutable in its substance though constantly changing in volume of circulation. Upon it all our inter-human transactions are based, our inheritances counted and our failures paid for.

Civilization is the name of this patrimony that men have learned to produce, and the know-how of its production is the distinctive attribute of the human race. An immemorial capital of skills accumulated against the resistance of physical nature and human nature, it has been transmitted and multiplied from generation to generation. The history of civilization is the history of the uninterrupted invention of organs all aimed at assisting the societies of men toward the release and utilization of the power that they make and by which they are made.

The circumstances of men's labor condition the freedom they derive from it; and the test of freedom is the degree of control men are able to exert on those circumstances. This has always been so; but as long as there were no world-wide economic forces whose impact reached all men, the release of the power that is freedom was the private affair of certain privileged groups or nations. In our time the machine, capitalism and democracy offer freedom a range as broad as the world we live in; or they can make for universal chaos and slavery, which ultimately means fascism.

Fascism was the attempt to curb all men under a discipline of obedience from which they could never again emerge with any degree of independence. Evil men have always tried to smash the dynamism of freedom at the juncture of obedience and independence. They have done this in two ways: by crushing men into modes of obedience from which there could be no recovery, and by stirring their emotions with dreams of boundless independence. Old-time tyrants always tried to do both these things. But they never had at their disposal such instruments of pressure and incitement as are available to modern dictators. Tyrants never had electronics at their service. They never had the opportunity that fascism enjoyed: that of finding large masses of men at the exact moment when they knew how to use new and revolutionary tools of production but had not yet learned to master those tools for their own benefit.

Fascism came at a time when the understanding of freedom had been marred by dangerous misconceptions. We had grown to believe freedom meant that men were entitled to act and live and think according to the dictates of their whims. We had been told it could be claimed and enjoyed by impersonal groups, by nations or classes, with the individual completely submerged. On all sides, men had been tempted to tear apart the essential elements of the dynamism of freedom and to conceive of freedom without work, of independence without obedience, of obedience without independence, of the individual detached from society, or of society as an end in itself. It was a time of great heresies.

So the greatest of all heresies became possible—that of organizing merciless modes of life and work where the worker must remain worker forever, chained to his job and his class, without hope of reaching any measure of independence or privacy. The implication was that men do not need to do their work well and that the power of a community can be multiplied by multiplying the obedience of its citizens. The raw labor of enslaved men was thought to be enough·for what a mechanical civilization demands.

The measure of independence men gain is something they ransom with the work of their lives. Fascism tried to crush the idea of a ransomed independence, and set itself to destroy the religions that have taught men how to redeem themselves with their work. ·

Fascism went under because it was wrong—the unwinding of civilization that brings mankind back to the condition of the herd. But other misconceptions are still with us. Communism is the most widespread of these—the most ominous, should it succeed either in dominating the world or in making the rebirth of fascism inevitable. Paradoxically, it may prove the most healthy, if under its attacks the men who believe in freedom regain awareness of their own strength.

Communist doctrine maintains that because the circumstances of men's labor determine their political order, men can reach a secure and permanent condition of freedom only by entrusting to the state the ownership of the means of production. To reach this goal, the people, the so-called proletariat, must establish their dictatorship over their countries, a dictatorship exercised by a group of men who claim to be the best possible accountants of the people's investments and needs.

Communism is quite correct in pointing out that there is a relationship between conditions of labor and political freedom. But it does not go far enough; in fact it only goes half of the way. It takes into account that part of the process of production that brings about the absorption of men in their labor, but leaves out the other part which concerns the release of the laborer from his labor. It confiscates or at least indefinitely suspends the enjoyment of personal independence, the emergence of man from the obedience and anonymity of work. It presumes to short-cut the whole process of accumulation of experience, growth of personality, re-investment of work, entrusting it to the care of self-perpetuating totalitarian rulers.

This is an orgy of half-truths, for the relationship of men to their instruments of production is only half understood if we think that all it demands of them is to give more and more of themselves to the productive process.

The other half of the cycle is concerned with producing not things or services, but persons.

In our Western societies the results of the fission between labor and freedom can be seen broadly unfolded in two different and related sets of institutions. One is called economics, the other politics. One is focused on the production and distribution of goods and services, the other on the use or misuse that men make of the freedom they gain out of their work. One in concerned with the subject matter of their labor, the other with their capacity for emerging from it and going beyond it, in a broader sphere of association and opportunity than the one defined by the strict conditions of work. One gives them tools for obedience; the other, tools for independence. Men earn their freedom in the places where they work, but they spend it or are robbed of it in their communities. In a free society, the citizen consoles the worker.

Politics is the answer men give to the conditions of their lives. It can be the organization of their opportunity to gain a measure of independence from their work with a view to improving their condition; or it can be a system of deceptive compensations organized in the interest of a few individuals who have robbed the people of this opportunity. Politics organizes either the manipulation or the confiscation of the freedom that the people make.

Politics is men's answer to economics. We use and exchange in our communities the independence we gain with our work. Frequently we are short-changed. In our factories, in our workshops or at our desks, we may bring some improvement in the conditions of our obedience, but we can hardly escape the bitter taste of obedience. Through the instruments of politics we find the practical tokens of whatever freedom we have achieved, or we have no freedom at all. Through politics the citizen, together with other citizens or in competition with them, may enjoy what freedom is his. But this enjoyment is a fraud if it is dispensed by self-appointed wardens on the basis of their own accounting and planning.

For freedom, although made only by individuals, is the most social and socializing of all products, the most communicative, the most widely understood and the most irrepressible. No man or group of men may aspire to control the whole cycle of production, by-passing the individual for the sake of or with the prospect of an ultimate boundless enjoyment. No social organ or political body can take over from the individual his task and privilege of squaring out at the end of a day or a job what he has done and what has been done to him, what he can do next and what he can do better in the broad society in which he lives.

Political freedom guarantees the emergence of the worker from the anonymity and the drudgery of work. It is the surplus profit of the laborer, whose reward is not adequate when it is represented merely by a pay envelope or by a coupon redeemable at a company or state-owned store.

In a communist form of society this surplus profit is confiscated. In the forms of society we call democratic, it is haphazardly and sometimes wastefully collected. The condition for the victory of democracy over its opponents is that the collection be set right.

CHAPTER II

THE NATURE OF RIGHTS

"We, the peoples of the United Nations, determined ... to re-affirm faith in fundamental human rights, in the dignity and worth of the human person, in the equal rights of men and women and of nations large and small . . ." So the preamble of the UN Charter reads. And the Atlantic Charter gives us freedom of speech, of press, from want and fear, as the fundamental rights of every man and woman "everywhere in the world." Yet immediately after Hitler's fall furious controversies began between the Western powers and Soviet Russia over the rights of free speech and press and "unfettered" elections. Each one of these rights, while held to be valid everywhere in the world, has been flouted or violated by the major powers in many parts of the world. Actually, in the wide-open market of international affairs the rights of small nations are objects of lively bargaining.

The fact is that for too long a time our thinking about rights and freedoms has been a dim reverberation of ideas that our fathers used to cherish. The founders of this country, like their enlightened European contemporaries, strongly believed in nature's rights. We have kept the verbiage and the ceremonial of that faith. But verbal ad-

herence to the old principle of the rights of nature appears
to have absolved us from paying adequate attention to the
nature of rights.

There was a time when the rights of men were conceived as grants of power received from a benevolent deity
in order that men might toil for the salvation of their souls.
The faithful had to act upon their individual share of the
divine inheritance if they wanted to secure their future in
eternity. In this they were guided by the Church, which
during their station on earth gave constant warning and
foretaste of the life eternal.

There was a time when rights were conceived as the
gift of a benevolent nature that granted to all men opportunity for happiness, progress and enduring well-being. If
only man were wise enough correctly to interpret nature,
nature herself could be the universal guide of his behavior.

But in our day there are large numbers of men over
whom the idea of God has lost its sway, and among those
who do believe in God there are many who prefer to hide
their belief in their hearts and test their faith through their
work. Today we find it hard to think of nature as a kind
mother to men, and the more we learn the more skeptical
we grow about our own human nature. It is hard to believe in universal inalienable rights when we see the condition, in many parts of the world, of the supposed bearers
of these rights.

Still we go on making lists of rights that the United
Nations should some time establish. We draw new freedoms from the goodness of our hearts as we draw new
rights for nations large and small from our willingness
to give away our neighbors' empires. We make of our
present and future bills of rights the statement of our

laudable intentions, and if we feel sometimes that it may be difficult to put all of them into practice, we are reassured by the thought that they set high standards and that there is nothing wrong in being the well-wishers of a future better world.

But rights are not windfalls of philanthropy. They are the skills that men have developed in the production of freedom, for our rights give us the experience, the ability, to produce freedom out of our basic types of work.

When we do our work well, recover the energy we have invested, increase our personal power, we are not the first to undergo such an experience: we augment a social patrimony of which we have received the use, we improve on skills of which we are the beneficiaries. Work well done brings us into the community of those who did good work before us and whose performance has made our efforts possible. We gain some measure of freedom largely because countless men, long before we were born, and countless other men around us, known and unknown, contributed toward the creation of an enormous pool of human skills and disciplined power.

The efforts of those men who during fifty centuries created learning have become our right to an education. Three centuries of the development of physical sciences has given all men a claim to that well-being that those sciences can produce. What has been created but is far too great for the personal enjoyment or the vain satisfaction of the creators, what remains and grows thereafter but cannot become the restricted property of any individual or group or nation—that is the spring of our rights. Edison contributed more to the rights of man than Jefferson.

The spring of our rights is a surplus of power, of that mode of power which is freedom that can never be exhausted by those who release it but overflows and reaches other men, stimulating the release of their own power. The very fact that some men have attained a measure of freedom proves to other men that they may attain some further measure of freedom. The "Why me?" of the strong man made humble by his achievements, the "Why not me?" of men made ambitious by the example that has been set—this is at the spring of our rights. It is the evidence of the communal, social and socializing power of freedom.

Each right is based on a large stock of active human experience and demands a constant replenishing and increasing of that stock. Each right we enjoy is the result of long and specific exertion and demands constant renewal and multiplication of that exertion.

The right of free speech is the result of much skillful use of speech. The best way to defend it is by using speech as an instrument of understanding and communication, not for the fostering of ignorance and prejudice. When speech is used well, then it becomes an instrument of freedom. Its test is its ability to promote communication among men. The same can be said of any other right. The right of free press or assembly, for example, depends on how well basic issues are clarified by the instrumentality of the press or procedural rules of assembly. Freedom of speech, of education, of religion, does not mean that each one of these particular activities is thrown open for promiscuous unregulated use. Rather, it means that it is available to everybody willing to subject himself to the discipline that the particular activity demands and that makes of it a carrier of freedom. Free speech is promoted by the kind of speech that makes men free.

The right to profess a religion, which is called freedom of religion, does not mean a cynical indifference to religion or unrestrained license granted to any religious cult. Religious freedom is a mode, a type, of religious experience. The very belief in it implies a religion, a religion to which all faiths minister. It is based not on the equivalence of every possible religion, but upon reciprocal respect among those of them that hold like views of the sameness of human destiny. It is the high achievement of men who live a faith so well that they are able to join hands with other men who live the same experience through different media of mystical communication.

There is possibly no more delicate right than that of religious freedom, constantly endangered by cynicism on one side and bigotry on the other. When we gain freedom of religion, when we make of our faith a vehicle and a guarantee of freedom, then we run the risk of losing religion, of considering all major forms of belief as practically equivalent emotional outlets for simple people. When religious freedom turns into religious indifference, then new cults are likely to come into existence carrying all the earmarks of bigotry, and religion becomes again, as in its savage origin, a discipline of segregation.

Strangely enough, although to reach freedom through religion is difficult, it is not half so difficult as to reach religion through freedom, to re-invest in religion and re-express through religion that broader poised view of ourselves and of our neighbors that we gain when religion gives us media of communication with our fellow men. Tolerance evaporates easily into indifference, strength of belief into laxity. The moment when such a mode of activity as religion or thought is proclaimed free is frequently the moment when the sustained effort that had given that activity its discipline is relaxed. For freedom of religion is an exacting form of religion, just as freedom of thought demands unrelenting intellectual discipline.

Freedom of thought rapidly turns into freedom from sustained thinking unless there is a constant effort to expand and consolidate the realm of reason and check its rules. In the same way, freedom of religion can turn into freedom from religion. These long-stored patrimonies of thinking and believing are rapidly exhausted when the effort they demand is not sustained.

Our rights bring us the patrimony, the trust, that comes to us from past generations. This patrimony does not exactly belong to us, but we are dependent on it, in the sense that our mode of existence is determined by our inheritance and by the use we make of it. It is a legacy whose full benefit we may acquire by doing specific work, a legacy which determines our range of choice and initiative in the work to be done and gives us increasing benefits according to our capacity for doing that work well. But it is a wasted legacy when men are forbidden to use what is available to them or when they are told that they may enjoy it simply on presentation of their birth certificate.

A right always expresses a dynamic and functional relationship. It denotes an individual claim to the use of a certain amount of social power, a claim re-enforced by what society demands of the individual and realized according to the use the individual makes of his power. But we can never consider as a grant of a benevolent nature what is actually an ever-changing dynamic relationship between man and man, and between man and his heritage.

It is the function of rights to lift the individual to the point where he can do his work well, where he has a chance of becoming really an individual, a person, a bearer and maker of freedom. Rights bring the immemorial experience of freedom within the reach of each living man so that he too may have a chance to make the best of himself.

The measure of freedom we gain gives us a measure of equality. Since freedom is the common denominator of all our inter-human transactions, the measure of equality to be found in any given society is proportionate to the freedom produced. There was very little sense of equality in the world when men started emerging from their work and the peculiarities of their existence, learned to filter the results of their experience through their consciences, and civilization began.

There is little sense of equality among slaves and of freedom among children. Only the free and the adult can be equal, for they find in the measure of freedom that they conquer the common denominator of their different experiences, and in the exercise of their rights the common discipline that their activities demand. It is difficult to know whether all men are born free and equal, but certainly all have in their rights the instruments to achieve their own measure both of freedom and of equality. There is no real communication or fellowship among men unless there is a constantly reawakened and broadened sense of equality; and there is no equality unless there is production of freedom and no production of freedom unless there is work. The whole process is dynamic and hazardously creative.

For such creativeness, rights give us increasingly refined and complex skills. They keep proportion and communication among men, they energize the individual so that he may produce his fullest measure of freedom and equality. They are the condensers and transformers of the power of freedom, and by galvanizing the individual they generate the energy by which they are sustained.

A list of rights or bill of rights is not a pattern of time-less perfection valid for every place and every people. Rather, it is like an index of national income, subject to constant change through the fluctuation of rates of production and consumption. The rights of man are different as the heritages from the past and the conditions of life and labor are different. Moreover, they are different because the reality of rights lies not in their legal or philosophical formulation but in what men do with them.

No state or super-state can legislate for all men the identical enjoyment of basic rights or freedoms, any more than it can guarantee them the same degree of happiness or well-being. We cannot assume that every individual, just because he is an individual, has the capacity to use every right. We do not say that man is water-borne or air-borne. But we can say that man—this earth-bound animal—has learned and can learn to navigate and to fly.

There is one and only one right to which all men have an absolute and identical claim. It is the right to earn rights. Whenever the attempt is made to segregate any group of human beings because of race or of class or of religion and to put beyond their reach the basic skills that make men, then we can always know with absolute certainty that we are facing a most vicious form of evil—an evil that we must uncompromisingly fight. For it is just as murderous to deprive men of the capacity to reach their own measure of humanity as it is to massacre them.

The right to earn rights is a life-making right when respected, life-breaking when violated. It is the one and only right that is absolutely universal and binding for all men. Whoever violates it is an outlaw, a criminal against mankind, for this is the one and only article of universal legislation from which all our laws depend and which no law can proscribe.

Of course, violations of this one law occur every day, even in nations that have subscribed the charter of the United Nations. Ours are the times marked by new perfection in physical as well as in political genocide. But ours are also the times when we have learned how to vanquish and we are learning how to curb the outlaws.

CHAPTER III

THE DYNAMISM OF RIGHTS

T HAT RIGHTS are not inalienable but can be alienated and lost, the experience of our time has proved beyond any reasonable doubt. If we abuse them, if we are flippant and careless in their use, if we rely on an inexhaustible margin of tolerance to cushion our failures and mistakes, we find that our great inheritance can end in total bankruptcy.

The price we have to pay for an obsolete conception of rights is heavy, as we know now when we see the rights of democracy claimed by those who, like the communists, do not care for freedom. We are at a loss then, torn between the temptation to make enjoyment of democratic rights conditional upon a belief in freedom, and our own confusion as to what actually constitutes the essence of this belief.

We face the communists' challenge in every field of political competition, in the internal politics of the countries in which we live and in the bodies and organs of the United Nations. We denounce the falsity of the communists' claims when they dare to call *free* the elections in countries where the citizen has no margin of privacy and no opportunity for choice, or when they claim that their own communistic order is a newer and more perfect form of democracy. But we cannot combat falsehoods with obsolete, half-forgotten truths. Neither can we hope to outdistance our communist opponents by setting up universal bills of rights which they are bound to violate and which we cannot enforce. If we are aware of the power that is on our side, we will have nothing to fear from any opponent—but this awareness requires a detailed objective knowledge of our own power.

Only knowledge can guide us to a better use of our rights, knowledge of their laws and their dynamism, of what makes for their waste and loss and of what we can do to make them more real. To become freer and stronger we do not need to discover new patterns of living and new ideologies; we have only to be alert and obedient to the forces that sustain us.

We are not accustomed to think of freedom and rights as a whole. Like children, we fix our attention upon the more obvious and pleasant features which we arbitrarily wrench from their context. We regard our rights as somebody else's business, run for our personal profit. Instead of considering freedom as high-tension energy, we see it as something boundless, shapeless and disembodied, something exalted and rare, that very few men and possibly no man can enjoy.

In the same way we are accustomed to think of rights as grants received from God or nature or popular will, and not as an inner discipline, a historically rooted and constantly growing social experience. In fact, we have been willing to give our rights for safekeeping to any self-appointed representative of God or nature or popular will who promised us increasing returns.

So by taking the position of the individual in the dynamism of rights out of context, some people who call themselves liberals have made it an end in itself, unrelated to the past or to the society in which the individual lives. While it is true that rights give the individual an opportunity to live his life more fully, to live a life that is his and only his, they at the same time require that he contribute to his time and place the energy with which they have provided him.

The more pointed our skill and the greater the range of our power, the more are we agents of something bigger than ourselves. Our "I" grows according to the competence it develops in us as agent and trustee for other human beings. This "I" does not mean a socially tolerable range of lawlessness that is legitimate as long as it is harmless to others. It means the holding of a trust.

Each one of us is more or less of a person according to his capacity for molding into a unity the fragments of experience he happens to live through. Rights work for order and for the narrowing of accidents so that our personality may have a chance to shape itself. But they do not make of our "I" a little isolated God; rather they give us a chance to justify and ransom ourselves. The greater and the more profitable to ourselves the use we make of this chance, the greater our responsibility becomes. The more power we hold, the less we own it. Complete ownership, unrestrained and unreserved, were it to exist anywhere in our day, could be only the little pleasure of little people.

There has been a tendency in the so-called liberal school of thought to focus attention on the secondary and peripheral aspects of freedom rather than on its hard core of sustained, concentrated energy. Thus it has been insisted that to be free means to be able to make a choice between alternatives, that to enjoy political freedom means to be able to choose between different programs of government. This has some elements of truth, provided we remember the amount of work required to clear up the complexities, the uncertainties, of a given social situation before we can face it in terms of reasonable alternatives.

We like to select a comfortable and dramatic moment of the dynamism of freedom, and we think of that moment as the essence or the whole of it. We even make of the right to choose the test of all our rights, while actually the element of choice is but the crowning feature in the process of freedom, the moment when by making a decision we reap the harvest of countless other decisions and efforts. But freedom is not Hamlet's dilemma, nor is it a constant limping from one dilemma to another. When we test the skills we have inherited and improve on them, we are not making choices all the time. We are doing things and testing our power. Freedom does not live on uncertainties: it clears up uncertainties. And we do not prove our freedom when we face but when we make a choice.

There is a pause of indifference, a time for rest, between the various phases of our work. We need rest to absorb the impact of what we have done, to emerge from our fatigue, to re-acquire some mastery over ourselves. When we are through with our job we take leave of what we have done. Sometimes it is difficult to know when a job is over, sometimes we do not know when to take leave, sometimes we take too extended a leave and we are lost. During our pauses of indifference we are inclined to be so tolerant of other tendencies and attitudes that we are likely to make our tolerance wholesale and blind. Again, this is an isolated moment in the dynamism of freedom—a moment during which much waste occurs. But it is not the whole of freedom.

For there is no such things as universal indiscriminate tolerance. Certainly it is not a right. Should it exist, it would mean the dissipation of all rights. The speech of wise and responsible men makes harmless and bearable the gabble of the malicious and the silly. When religious freedom is actually a religion, then the cults of cranks and bigots are fairly harmless. Good work creates a margin of tolerance for bad work, and the size of this margin is determined by the amount of good work done. Every right operates as a form of group insurance extended to those who give their activity to a certain type of work. Within a craft the good workers protect a certain number of slackers.

Freedom of thought is founded on the extraordinary amount of well-done, disciplined thinking that has been produced throughout history. It is a powerful foundation that allows a very large margin for error. Good thinking helps to make bearable irresponsible and vicious thinking. But if we imagine that any margin of tolerance, in thinking or any other activity, is limitless and inexhaustible, then the time always comes when we realize that we have overdrawn on our rights. There is a justice, a strict accounting, in the balance sheet of each right which leaves little room for counterfeiting and chicanery.

While a flat, easygoing conception of rights has become prevalent, technology has drawn immeasurably large masses of men to uniform types of work and has immeasurably multiplied the power, the reach, of human labor. To an incredible degree it has socialized civilization and made it potentially accessible to all human beings. It has made rights increasingly universal and the skill they demand increasingly teachable. The peculiarity of modern times is that industrial civilization has imposed on all mankind, practically without regard to race, color, or sex, uniform types of labor and has made all these types of labor directly and immediately interdependent.

There was a time when only kings had rights, when all the major functions of civilizations, all the highest or key types of human activity, like politics, culture, religion, were the jealously guarded privilege of endowed groups of knights or priests. But a trend of evolution that began with Christianity and reached its explosive climax with industrialism has gradually popularized all of the most exclusive and strategic types of craftsmanship. Rights have been popularized because the types of labor on which the crafts were founded were popularized. This fact, far more than any ideology, is the basis of modern democracy.

We have seen attempts made to bring back old racial or class restrictions in our time and to return the enjoyment of rights to a selected few. These reactionary attempts were possible because sight was lost of the nature and function of rights.

It was thought that the discipline of the main types of labor was a purely technical or rather technological matter. It was thought that the principles of mechanical engineering, combined with those of bookkeping, were enough to give us the direction we needed in the conduct of our business ventures. But the discipline of our types of labor —if labor is not to be slavery—lies in our rights, and the function of rights is to help and guide the production of that particular by-product of labor that is freedom. It was thought that machines could do the whole job and that the flow of production by itself could guarantee order and happiness in the world. It was an unfortunate thought, because the production of freedom is the job of men, not of robots.

Industrial civilization, by calling upon increasingly large masses of men to give their measure of exertion and obedience, has sharply revealed the inner structure of our system of rights. The dynamism of production, far from replacing or outdating the dynamism of rights, has at the same time energized and exposed it. The system of rights has made the dynamism of production irrepressible; but unleashed production turns into a curse, unless it is directed to strengthen the system of our rights.

The popularization of skills, the fact that in spite of their complexity they became accessible to increasingly large masses of human beings, is the final achievement of a long series of efforts throughout history. It came from the hard work done by men who conquered their measure of freedom from old prejudices or from a stubborn physical nature—men working in monks' cells or in parliaments or in scientific laboratories, or wrestling in jails with their own abjection and despair. These men gained their own specific measure of freedom, each following his own vocation, pushing ahead in his own way; for freedom is something that is gained in segments and worked out within bounds.

When industrial civilization brought the process to a climax, it made available to the many the results of the sacrifices and labors of the few. It created conditions that immeasurably extended the potential range and dimensions of human freedom. But of itself it does not provide freedom, no matter whether it is run for private or for collective profit.

Yet industrialism developed as a perfect image of the dynamism of rights. Like freedom, it proved so contagious that no nation, not even a barely civilized people, could avoid its impact. At times, under particularly favorable conditions such as those prevailing on the North American continent, it gave large masses of men an opportunity to improve their individual lot by their work. Like freedom, it satisfied on an ever-increasing scale the fundamental needs of men and awakened in them an awareness of more needs to be satisfied. Both industrialism and freedom draw their strength from the work of the individual, both create solidarities, conflicts and links among individuals, and both in order to keep going demand more work.

For the modern mode of production is something more than the result of lucky inventions or fortunate discoveries in the pursuit of human progress. Its dynamism is molded on the pattern, runs parallel to the laws, of the dynamism of rights. It reveals and gives full scope to all the inner features and potentialities of the dynamism of rights. Industrial civilization is the divulger of relationships and trends that used to be scattered, unrelated and hidden. It has made explicit and visible what was always there. Breaking the ties of prohibition and superstition, it has made economic production as self-expanding and self-sustaining as the life of the spirit became when men discovered in themselves the art of living it fully.

The fact that the road to industrialism was paved by such experiments and researches in freedom as Greek culture and the Jewish and Christian religions means that for more than three thousand years mankind has been undertaking experiments in universalism and individualism, learning how to shake off the doom of irrevocable destiny by working out for itself as much salvation and wisdom as it could. Long before universal systems of accounting were established, men in the Western world had acquired the habit of assessing their sins and virtues according to universal principles of bookkeeping. Indeed, it is strange that industrialism took so long to come into the world and to develop its full dynamism as a physical complement and outgrowth of the already thoroughly tested dynamism of rights.

The system of rights tends to establish a floor and a ceiling between which men may develop their work with the greatest possible degree of predictability as to the outcome of their efforts, and with the greatest possible limitation upon the role of blind chance. It is no accident that in our times the people everywhere ask now for social insurance in order that the role of blind chance in their lives be minimized; for a floor and a ceiling within whose limits their work can be developed and its outcome be made predictable. It is neither an accident nor due to theory that trade unions and workers' organizations have arisen everywhere and that with these new institutions the people assert their claim to benefits which the dynamism of rights provides and which now must be organized on the unprecedented dimensions that industrialism has created.

But the mechanical mode of production, whether run for private profit or for a communist society, does not by-pass the individual. It does not demand that in our thinking or in our mode of social living we imitate the machine. It cannot be detached from the moral Christian tradition to which it owes its origins without inevitably boomeranging against man.

Freedom is exacting and there can be no cheapening of it or substitute for it. Its immemorial power comes to us through our rights, which train us to perform in the best possible way the main activities and functions on which civilization depends. All such functions and needs—thinking and producing and believing—can be instrumental in the production of freedom, which is a piecemeal, not a wholesale, job. We work out our measure of freedom a fragment at a time. We are made that way. We cannot pretend to live life. We live as fully as we can that fragment of life that is our own life.

Like the forces of the physical world that man gradually uncovers, learns to obey as laws and to use for his own purposes, rights are the forces and laws of the human world that men have made. More than three thousand years of hard work and tireless patience have gone into the discovery of the laws of physical nature, and industrialism finally became possible. Industrialism has repaid the service by exposing the structure of our rights and the claim that all men have upon them.

We do not get electric power simply out of the air or in water or in a pile of coal. Man has to apply his ingenuity in devising machines and in running them properly if he wants to capture the forces of nature and satisfy his needs. The same applies to the forces and the laws of the world that men have made. We can never hope to satisfy our ever-increasing needs without knowing how to master the complex and difficult tools of political organization.

The acknowledgment of the universal needs of the human person and his "worth" cannot help the individual to defend and assert himself against the political and economic forces preying on him, any more than the acknowledgment of the law of gravity can determine the type of houses in which it is safe for us to live.

We need political organs for the harmonization of the dynamisms of production and rights. The two cannot be separated. The dynamism of rights has brought into existence the dynamism of production, the dynamism of production has prodigiously enlarged the scope of the dynamism of rights. The major political problem of our age is to establish the proper correlation between the two, so that the largest possible number of men may find in their own work the means to increase the power and to broaden the range of their freedom.

CHAPTER IV

THE RIGHT TO WORK

W E KNOW freedom when we do our work well. But what knowledge of freedom can those of us gain who have no work to do? And what kind of freedom can be recovered by those who have no particular incentive to do their work well—who simply sell and deliver a certain amount of raw energy for cash?

Mechanical civilization has affected people's lives everywhere on earth and has demanded work from everyone, regardless of race, sex or belief. But the very source of its power is in the hands of masses of men whose grasp of the institutions of freedom is hampered by the mode of their labor. The machines that impose their pace on our lives and determine our society are largely entrusted to men whose link with society is tenuous and precarious.

There is little that a manual or clerical worker can build on, and even less that he can consider really his own. He has his job—when he has a job—and he has his certificate of citizenship. In a democracy a certificate of citizenship gives one the right to organize and to vote, and the worker can improve the conditions of his life to the extent of gaining security in his job, more cash and less work. Politicians are always ready to assume the custody of a worker's electoral certificate.

The worker's standard of living may be at times comparatively high, and his trade union influential. Yet there are only two things he has to fall back on: his job and his citizenship. He spends the political advantage of his citizenship in order to protect his job; and his position, no matter how prosperous and influential it sometimes may be, is at the threshold of the political community, seldom deep inside it.

Each worker is limited to some infinitesimal segment of that endless line over which goods flow. With his own hands he makes things or converts them or registers their movements; but of the meaning of his work and its final disposal he has little or no conception. His energy remains vague and unblended, its outlet is rarely a specific job which can be well done, but merely a job. When large masses of workers are without work, then even those who have a skill are lost in the undifferentiated vagueness of the search for a job. When they do have work their obedience to it runs from day to day or week to week. Their independence cannot help but be as precarious as their obedience. There seems to be no way for them to recover the energy they release. They give it away in small installments, by the hour, by the day or by the week. They give it away irretrievably in exchange for a pay envelope.

This condition hardly makes for freedom. It is a condition where large masses of workers are citizens but not quite citizens, because they have to focus all their energies on the defense of what for them is the prerequisite of active citizenship—a job. And they are workers but not quite workers, because they have little chance of giving themselves to what they do and of doing it well. Rather, they are producers and deliverers of energy that the market requires. Mechanical civilization has recast the world and made a unity of it; yet at the very source of its power it operates by milking raw energy from isolated, uprooted men.

This condition does not make for freedom because freedom is a technique of labor; but the crude labor that the machine demands seems to be the least susceptible to handling by this technique. This anomaly is an infection that makes for more infection. The vagueness of marginal citizenship and unattached work calls forth the vagueness of revolutionary theorists who, like yes-men of evil, applaud the process and want to have all workers, manual and others, skilled and unskilled, equally unattached. It calls forth demagogues who go to the manual workers and tell them that they should be the masters, while other demagogues stir up fear of the workers in the rest of the community, in order to have the workers beaten into slavery.

Totalitarianism always begins its conquests either by attacking or by debauching the workers and their organizations. They do this because they know that the most vulnerable spot of a democratic society is there. There large masses of men are in a position of power because they work at or for the machines. Yet when they want to have their power recognized and feared, the best they seem able to do is to make the machines idle.

The workers consume their citizenship in order to protect their jobs and consume their jobs to implement their citizenship. This condition does not make for strength when, in the downgrade spirals of economic depression, their work is slowed down, jobs become scarce, and large masses of workers have no other way of making a living than by cashing in their citizenship for a relief job or a dole. Under all circumstances, employed or unemployed, during prosperity or depression, they have to struggle for their existence. But men who always struggle for their existence in the end gain nothing more than existence, even when they are successful.

Industrialism has done all this. It forced peoples to overcome countless barriers formerly imposed by religious or political customs, distance and time. It called in men of all social strata, all races, faiths and cultures, and taught them its easy-to-learn techniques. It enabled them to work according to new and revolutionary patterns that cross the boundaries of states and empires. But though it called all men to work, it seemed unable to provide them with steady work. At the cost of countless uprootings it grabbed each man and told him how to do a job, but it did not provide him with a secure job. It called all men, but it did not seem capable of absorbing all of man or of filling his heart.

The mechanical mode of production broadened the scope of our system of rights but at the same time threatened its foundations. It broadened the scope because it made all skills infinitely teachable and interrelated; it threatened the foundations because it demanded a type of labor which requires no skill. It is a type of labor that can be done by toilers, by men who are workers but not quite workers, citizens but not quite citizens, and whose position both as workers and citizens is insecure. Their unblended, undifferentiated labor gives a marginal value to their rights and to their citizenship. This situation threatens the debasement of all rights, because the marginal value of freedom determines its course.

As a principle this has always been true, but today it is relevant on a total scale. The impact of industrialism has completely abolished the proud seclusion of nations and races; there is no room in our world for private civilizations. Today for the first time in the history of man, civilization is available to all, because industrialism has created uniform tools that make this interdependent unity not only possible but actual. An automobile, a turbine, a complicated machine that even half-civilized men can learn to use, spills most of civilization's secrets and teaches the same language to all men. Today the principle that the marginal value of freedom determines its course operates instantly and irreparably.

Marxism teaches that the condition of the manual workers must ultimately and inevitably lead to their supremacy. On the contrary, the fact of their marginal, unattached status creates the condition for totalitarianism. Totalitarian regimes may be different and opposed to each other, but they all want to make of labor a discipline of segregation under which peoples must keep to their allotted places, grateful to the leading group for tolerating their physical survival. The mechanical mode of production has made toilers of the large majority of industrial workers. Totalitarianism deliberately makes toilers of all men not belonging to the leading group.

The problem with which industrialism confronts us and which industrialism by itself cannot solve is how to absorb the unattached workers into the community, how to recapture the energy now going to waste which threatens to rot the foundations of our society. Industrialism creates conditions that may make for democracy or for totalitarianism, but by itself it cannot counteract the debasing influence it exerts on the freedom of the workers.

Marxism offers no solution to this problem but, as Russian communism proves, only serves to aggravate it. Russian communism embitters the subjection of the workers by the mockery of a regime that pretends to be their own dictatorship. Communism is the aggravation of a disease that pretends to be its cure. It ignores the fundamental problem of finding a means by which the unattached worker can be absorbed in the community without destroying freedom in the community.

If the debasement of freedom is to be stopped, the workers must be in condition to attain the largest possible enjoyment of rights in spite of the mode of their labor. Labor has always been the raw material from which freedom grows. But it is a fallacy to believe that men can unfailingly recover independence from their labor, for the types of labor on which large masses of men now depend blunt their capacity to recover even a modicum of independence. Unless the debasing influence of the industrial mode of labor is counteracted by a new right, all modes of labor will be reduced to the aimlessness and insecurity of unattached work. This new right is called the right to work.

In our time the right to work has acquired an urgency above all other rights and appears as the foundation of them all. For it is not just the right to have a job, but to conditions of labor and compensations for labor that do not bar the enjoyment of other rights. Actually, the right to work has become the contemporary version of the right to earn rights.

If every man is to be guaranteed a job, if in every community we are to have full employment, we need also to provide that men emerge from their jobs, not be consumed

by them. Any totalitarian regime can guarantee full employment. But in order to secure the fundamental conditions that make freedom fully workable in our time, the
dynamism of freedom must operate with the greatest possible effectiveness. This is the paradox of our situation: we
must be free in order to establish freedom. We must put a
foundation under the house we live in.

To maintain democracy nationally and internationally
we need to have institutions that bring democracy within
reach of the workers. We must have the fullest and most
effective use of political democracy in order to establish
what is called economic democracy. Otherwise, in order
to gain the right to work we lose our other rights. And if
we lose our rights, we lose all.

A right is a claim on a certain measure of tolerance and
assistance from the community, a claim redeemed or for-
feited according to a man's participation in the life and
work of the community. The right to work is a man's
claim on his community by reason of the very conditions
of modern work; and in our time this claim is extended to
the larger community organized by modern modes of production—a community which stretches far beyond the
boundaries of any one of our states or empires.

Civilization can hardly survive unless the large masses
of men who have sunk to the lowest level of freedom are
given the opportunity to free themselves from want and
from fear. Yet no organization, whether national or super-
national, can become the monopolistic giver of work to
its citizenry without ultimately threatening the basis of
their humanity. Any government which attempts to take
over the function of freeing men from want and from
fear is likely to become the main cause of want and the
object of the most hopeless fear.

What workers need everywhere in the world is to have roots somewhere, to have a chance to incorporate their power in something over which they have some control, that belongs to them and to which they belong. They want to be men everywhere in the world, not condensers of manpower to be sold at retail, or mere items of accounting. They need to live under conditions where their fear may find its match in their strength and where they may become self-reliant enough to cope with the threat of want. Because ultimately man can be freed from fear only by his own heart, and from want only by the skill of his own hands.

The dynamism of rights tends to give men sturdy hearts and adroit hands, but unless men have work and are in a condition to derive freedom from their work, the process breaks down.

In order to counteract the odds against them and reach a collective strength equal to that of their employers, the workers organize themselves in trade unions. The experience of the last hundred years has shown that just as the right to work is the key right of our time, so freedom of the workers' organizations is the freedom on which all other freedoms hinge. When the workers' organizations are crushed or perverted, democracy is stabbed to the heart.

However, the trade union is so literally and almost mechanically the workers' answer to what factory or office work demands of them that its activity seldom extends to the broader causes of the workers' plight. By fencing the workers within their occupational organization, the trade union constantly runs the risk of redoubling their isolation from the rest of the community. It consolidates the position of the workers at the outskirts of the community, but rarely succeeds in bringing them into the community.

The function of the trade union to be adequate must be much broader than that. It must lift the workers out of their hypnotic absorption in the drab routine of their jobs and broaden the outlook of their lives; it must make citizens of them in spite of the drudgery of their work. The workers attain full citizenship when they draw out of their work not merely a pay envelope but a measure of usable political power. This is a compensation to which the industrial mode of labor entitles them. It can be spent within their trade unions to make them more truly representative and less boss-ruled; it can be spent in improving their lot in the factories where they work by means of co-operation with management and the establishment of reciprocal responsibilities; it can be spent in assuming a large measure of control over their protective organizations.

The movement has just started in this direction, and there is a very long way to go. The basic conditions of labor can be radically improved by such means as yearly wages, housing under workers' control and responsibility, political self-government on the part of the worker in what are still called company towns. All this, however, requires political alertness on the part of the individual worker rather than a supine obedience to the trade union boss or the communist agitator. For the extra measure of power to which the worker is entitled is lost, not only when he becomes the ward of a totalitarian party, but when he allows his group to become a petty tyrant of the general public. His plight is not relieved but aggravated when his trade union is so run that it must become either the slave or the master of the community.

The worker must be in a position to exert his full citizenship in the marginal zone in which he is placed by the necessities of modern industry and which is closest to his immediate experience. It is a new sphere of politics that under the new conditions of industrialism has largely assumed the basic, primary role that used to belong to municipal government. It is a sphere of politics that must be democratically organized by the workers in their organizations; and it is so vital that the whole structure of a democratic society is wrecked when the workers either try to by-pass it or are nailed to it. The political problem of labor is basic to our civilization and can wreck it if not adequately solved. However, its level is that of a badly overdue municipal reform, not of Armageddon.

Just as there is no loyalty to the larger national or international commonwealth unless there is a sense of and a care for the community which is closest to us, so the worker cannot fully participate in the political life of his nation unless he contributes an active citizenship to the organization in which he works and to those created to compensate him for the insecurity of his work. Without such participation, his political power remains as disembodied and unblended as his labor.

After the worker has become a citizen of his own community, then like any other citizen he will strive to reach as high a degree of political power as he can. But the first step is to feel a part of what he does, to live the life of the organization in which he spends his days, to find in his own immediate political life a compensation for his labor. Men need to feel a part of what they do, to have a share in it and be proud of it. They need it so desperately that sometimes, as communism has proved in Russia and outside Russia, they are driven to prefer a purposeful slavery to an aimless freedom.

CHAPTER V

THE GREAT HERESY

THE FACT that modern machines can relay such an enormous amount of power and do the job of such an amazing number of men has radically upset the relationship between men and their work. It has upset the political as well as the economic aspects of their relationship; men's attitude toward their commonwealths as well as toward their labor. Yet it was thought that what modern technology had subverted it could also automatically repair. It was thought that technological progress could provide a constant economic improvement destined to stimulate a constantly growing social harmony. It seemed to offer ever more power for limited investments of energy and a bountiful production of things designed to make men happy.

We have grown accustomed to living on the fat of that bounty, confident that by exploiting lucky breaks of invention we could go on working less and less and enjoying more and more. It was like having the advantages of an unlimited supply of slave labor, while avoiding the abjection of slavery in our midst.

Having found Eldorado in our labor-saving and power-multiplying machines, it was thought that the drudgery of running them and the toil of their accounting could be left to a comparatively small number of technicians and to a large shifting mass of industrial and white-collar workers. It was accepted as inevitable that these workers in pits, at desks or on assembly lines should be deprived of the conditions that make for happiness through work and of incentives to do their work well. They were consumers too, as well as tools of production, and by raising their wages or salaries high enough their increased purchasing power could bring the blessings of mechanical civilization within their grasp. The satisfaction of doing their work well as producers might be denied them, but they could find compensation as consumers of cheap goods and gadgets. Low-price markets, low-price entertainment and yellow journalism would provide convenient substitutes for freedom.

It was thought that the return on the appalling power of the machines could be counted in terms of increased profits and rising wages and salaries, with some disastrous cycles of depression in between. The economic organization of society seemed so perfect and was performing so many miracles that there appeared to be no reason why it could not take the place of politics, or at least reduce politics to a subsidiary branch of business. The people's answer to this state of affairs would be a demand for more and more goods, to be made available through more and more purchasing power. Mechanical civilization could satisfy this as well as any other need, at a lesser and lesser cost. The response of men to their economic condition did not need

to be very articulate or imaginative; all they had to do was
to say "yes," "more" and "me too."

We have been deluding ourselves with fragmentary
reasoning and fragmentary computation. One day we
could buy cheap gadgets and the next day we doubled
the cost by paying a dole to the laborers who made the
gadgets that we thought we had bought. One day our
nation was prosperous, its standard of living high, with
gold flowing to it from all over the world. The next day
we paid dearly in terms of wealth and blood because our
neighbors were suffering under a distress which the previous day we had thought was none of our business. There
seems to be something wrong with our system of accounting, our way of reckoning profit and loss.

We thought it was possible to use our machines for joy
rides and comfort. We thought what we had to pay for
them was merely the price indicated by the competitive
market, and eventually made easy by installment buying.
We thought we could use this gigantic power for the
benefit of lucky individuals and lucky nations. In fact,
we all wanted to be lucky and acted as if we had a right
to be—until something snapped in the world and civil war
came. Then we began to realize that we were just starting
to pay for the machines we thought we owned, for the
wealth we thought was ours, and that the sheriff was on
his way to take everything back.

We had become accustomed to drifting along on the
power we were releasing, and had lost the capacity to see
where we were being led. The fact was that we had never

mastered the power that came from the machines: we had simply plundered it. We had never really led the machines but had ridden along on their power. We thought that the relationship of men to their work could be solved by simply asking the machines what they wanted of men and that then they could run by themselves with the happiest possible automatism.

There was an attempt to let business do the whole job of organizing society. Leave business men alone, it was said, let them take care of the production and distribution of wealth, free from governmental or political interference. They know that all men are both producers and consumers, and all that is needed is to accelerate production and spread consumption. In prosperous times the people were led to think that security meant plenty of cash and an immediate prospect of more cash. This was called freedom of the individual. By some it was even called liberalism.

There was the attempt to revolutionize society by eliminating private ownership of the means of production and giving all powers to the state. Politics, it was maintained, was just the façade of the economic framework. Once public ownership of the means of production had been established, men would have no need to question the direction in which they were driven and no urge to disentangle themselves from their work. The direction could be planned and determined mathematically, the bookkeeping of power could account for its course, and administration of things could replace government of men.

Finally there was the attempt, more radical and farther reaching than the others, to suppress at its source all possible groping toward personal independence. An iron discipline was to be imposed on society, a discipline that would discourage men from ever attempting to raise their heads, indeed from even conceiving that they had a right to their own lives.

All three attempts, economic liberalism, marxism and fascism, different as they are in origin and orientation, have something basic in common. They try to eliminate the function of politics, the watchful control by the people over the conditions of their own lives. The elimination is brought about by slow, sweet atrophy, by revolutionary upheaval or by cruel sterilization. Each of the three is designed to ride on the power released by machines and each is confident that it is following the correct interpretation of what machines demand of men. Each has as its aim the elimination of whatever is regarded as an obstacle in the way of an ultimately irresistible automatism.

Fascism that still exists somewhere in our world looks to a blind unleashing of power and a total elimination of all brakes. It has created no new forms of political organization but fanatically underscores the old loyalty of man to the state of which he is a citizen. It uses the typical institutions of a modern state—trade unions, schools, organs of social assistance—to turn men into unresisting tools of its will. These old social machineries have in them unsuspected reserves of efficiency and speed when they are used to keep man down. Three hitherto separate branches of technology—industry, politics and the military—can be amalgamated; the technocrats of unified power have only to speed up the process. The day will come, they think, when this mode of labor and life will take so much of the marrow of men that there will no longer be a need to whip them into obedience.

Fascism carries to its ultimate extreme the fundamental weakness which marxism and economic liberalism share.

According to their particular emphasis, all three systems offer different interpretations of one half of the productive process, the strictly economic technological aspect, and advocate three variant substitutes for political freedom. All have automatism as their aim. The political controversies of our time are conflicts between different blends of automatism and anarchism.

Anarchy is the common goal—an anarchy that economic liberalism conceives as healthy, that socialism looks upon as the final achievement of a thoroughly mechanized society and that fascism stirs up as the constant companion of its merciless discipline. All three *isms* are variant names for anarchy, which is the absence of man-devised, purposeful rules; all three are devices aimed at satisfying the longing for automatism.

Our attitude toward the power of rights has been the same as our attitude toward the power of industrial civilization. We have lived on our rights, taking the enjoyment of them for granted, just as we have lived on the fat of industrialism. We have made a fetish of technology, just as we have made a fetish of civil liberties.

Whenever the shortcomings in the application of our rights have been too glaring, whenever an ugly reality was flung in the face of our rhetoric, we always found handy justification in the thought that it was not easy, in fact not even possible, to reach a perfect, ideal fulfillment of rights and freedom. Similarly, economic depressions and large-scale unemployment were condoned as imperfections in the mechanism of production and distribution.

Having placed the "ideals" high in the skies of unattainable perfection, the way was paved for all sorts of compromises, for half-hearted or half-cynical adjustments that unfortunately fall far short of "perfection." We bore

with a sort of apologetic bad conscience the structure of
our civil liberties, feeling uneasy and self-conscious toward
the limitations they still imposed. Thus basic restrictions
on freedom of speech were conceived not as the discipline
that makes freedom real, but as painful concessions to
human frailty. By refusing to regard our civil liberties as
tools for the creation of positive freedom, we were
stopped from bettering them.

For the test of rights is not their approximation to a
so-called ideal, but the degree to which they succeed in
keeping proportion and communication among men. The
"ideal" is the death trap of all rights.

The ideal of freedom has too often been used to replace
freedom with lawlessness—a lawlessness that the mechanical
mode of production is supposed not only to render harmless but to reward with unending bounties.

Ideal freedom has been conceived as something boundless and shapeless, motionless and unattainable. Being unattainable by reason of the frailty of human nature, it could
yet be replaced on earth by some minor freedoms whose
number could be multiplied *ad infinitum*. High and aloof
as the Jewish God, it somehow countenanced a large and
growing number of inferior deities. Thus we had freedom
of the employee and of the employer, of nations and of
races. "Perfect" or "ideal" freedom, everyone knew, was
something no one could reach on this earth.

But freedom is not boundless or motionless or shapeless. It is the product of the dynamic relation of men to
their work, to their institutions and to one another. It is
always pointed, always identified with a particular subject

and borne by a particular subject. It is never disembodied but is related to the peculiarities and limitations of its individual carriers. It is not slackness but power. It is not an ideal but a fact, and the most powerful leavener of facts.

All the great religions of the West are based on a certain relationship between men and their God, with a margin of responsible action left to the individual. The modern attitude toward freedom is an apostasy from the basic beliefs of the West. It pays lip service to freedom, but places it so high, makes it so unattainable, that the best one can do is to drift along and hope that the drifting, thanks to mechanical civilization, may be as harmless as it is assumed to be rewarding.

Anarchy made safe and prosperous by modern technology, this seems to have been the steady goal. Ideologies pointed the way, each spearheaded by its *ism*, each seeking to eliminate politics and to find substitutes for freedom according to its own type of robot thinking.

And finally the mad revolt against Christianity came, against the idea of Christ as the highest power humbly embodied in human form. The Jewish people were made to pay very dearly for having borne Christ. When Hitler came, the mad revolt, aimed at making freedom of the human person at the same time meaningless and unattainable, finally denounced itself.

The exit of the greatest heretic and the defeat of the most heretical power have not eradicated heretical modes of thinking. Economic liberalism and marxism, having survived fascism, are gripped in what seems to be a fight to the finish. Once before, out of their struggle, fascism

came. In our days the major obstacle to a full-scale return
of fascism is the still-fresh memory of fascism.

On the other hand, perhaps one day economic liberalism
and marxism might come to tolerate each other and share
the world between themselves, finding in their common an-
tagonism toward freedom a bond of unity. Perhaps they
are not as much at variance as people think.

Just as we knew during the war that there could be no
compromise with the great heresy, so we should know
now that no peace can be built on a compromise between
lesser heresies. The road is long and hard, but the starting
point is to denounce and uproot the fallacies in our thinking. What we need most is to understand politics, the role
and the limit of politics, because it is only through the
workings of political institutions that freedom can be sal-
vaged.

For freedom is not something that men may have or not
have, according to chance or desire. It is what made and
makes man. It is to man what beauty is to art, and the
production of freedom is the destination and the test of
man, just as the achievement of beauty is the destination
and the test of art.

This has always been so, ever since the inestimable
treasures of civilization began to be accumulated for us.
But in our time the highest achievements of our Greek-
Hebrew-Christian inheritance, energized and spread by
industrialism, have become available to men in the mass.
The maker of freedom is, as it has always been, the individual. But today the release of the greatest amount of
freedom by the largest number of individuals has become
the condition for the survival of civilization everywhere.
Today freedom has become, not only for a selected few
but for mankind as a whole, what beauty is to art.

PART III

POLITICS

CHAPTER I

THE LIMITS OF POLITICS

W E WANT PEACE, but a peace purposefully organized and characterized by something better than the absence of war. It must be a peace that demands a greater and greater release of freedom within nations and among nations, a peace that disproves communism and gradually eliminates the causes that make for communism.

It must be the kind of peace that outlaws fascism and keeps it outlawed, for fascism is the extreme of all political heresies, the one that civilization can neither profit by nor endure. As freedom is the positive point of orientation from which to take our bearings, so fascism is the negative pole. We have now, as never before in history, the means to chart our course.

The last war engulfed a larger number of men than did any previous war in history. If a new war should come, it would engulf all men and take everything from them. It is not war in itself that is unendurable to this hardened human race, but the total type of war which grows out of fascism and makes for fascism. It is not the evil of tyranny in itself that is unendurable, but the irresistibly contagious, totalitarian fascist tyranny which is the suicidal answer to communist totalitarianism. We need a peace that leaves some limited room for the privacy of nations and of individuals—room even for the privacy of circumscribed evil and limited wars.

The peace we must build cannot pretend to answer the totalitarianism of fascism or of communism by bringing into the world total peace and total freedom. We have gone through too disastrous an experience with boundless totality. What we need now are measurable institutions and circumscribed ideas, shaped according to the wants and skills of men.

There is no full and immediate escape from total war and tyranny to total peace and freedom. We cannot hope to correct the evils of governments and sovereignty by organizing the world sovereignty of a world government. This is not a time for miracles. It is a time for purposeful, well-oriented political work. We must break the backbone of every totalitarianism, tyrannical or democratic, if we want to have institutions we can control.

Our aims must be at the same time exceedingly narrow and exceedingly far reaching. Since fundamental relationships are out of joint, we must fasten the sway of interests, passions and ideas to solid hinges. There is the relationship of men to their work, which is called the right to work or the problem of full employment; there is the relationship of the workers' political rights to the new conditions of industrial civilization, which is the problem of their active citizenship in the factory and in the community; and finally there is the relationship and reciprocal limitation of power among sovereign states. These are the main hinges that must be set straight by sustained political thought and political action. They demand precision work, not sweeps of rhetoric. We must reset the doors of the Temple of

Janus before we can start thinking of how and if and when they can be locked.

We cannot ask too much of this peace because we have to concentrate most of our energies on redrawing the boundary line between war and peace, armed warfare and politics. We cannot make much of this peace because we must start by salvaging and consolidating the terrain on which peace can be built. We cannot indulge in too much wishful thinking about the political work of the United Nations because we must acquire a basic feeling and a specific knowledge of what politics is and of how we can use it to organize peace.

Politics is and has always been an imitation of war aimed at exorcising war. It is a technique modeled on that of war, by which men and nations further their interests and measure their strength, using methods other than those of physical struggle. Through politics, conflicts among groups which seek to rule their country, or among countries which seek to defend their interests and ambitions, are resolved without violence. Through politics, men can learn to use ballots instead of bullets, symbols instead of weapons.

In their relationship with one another within an organized community, men learned long ago how to deal with violence and how to treat individuals who disregard the law or take it in their own hands. Such actions are called crimes and the individuals criminals. The community cannot undo a crime and cannot be satisfied with the punishment or the destruction of the criminal. The bad precedent must be erased lest the crime become a precedent and a law unto itself. To this end, in certain places called tribunals, and with a highly theatrical ceremonial, all the leftovers of the crime are assembled and the crime itself re-enacted. This time the law is not caught by surprise. All the elements that entered into the crime are present: the alleged criminal, the passions of the parties, those who witnessed the crime or suffered by it. The people too are present, the officials of the organized community and some random representative of the citizenry. Upon this re-enactment of the crime, into this setting where all interests and passions are at the same time keyed up and restrained, the sword of justice that once was caught off guard falls with all its weight. It is the execution in effigy of the crime.

Among political groups outbursts of violence are called revolution; among nations they are called wars. However, the technique of the execution in effigy works better when the alleged criminals are few, and the precedent established by the crime thus easily erased. Its regulated solemnity is difficult to introduce into the field of internal politics, where promoters of an unsuccessful revolution are to be punished; and still more difficult in the field of international conflict, where a whole nation of men would be in the dock. Yet when the abominations of the German people had somehow to be condoned, the technique of the criminal trial was employed at Nuremburg. Thus, with a supreme act of mercy, did the conscience of mankind attempt to place within a familiar human category the immeasurable beastliness of the Nazis.

The ceremonials of constitutional law have long tried to circumvent or discount revolution and civil war. The ceremonials of international law have tried to do the same for external war. Civilization is a constant quest for non-violent means of solving conflicts; it is a constant quest for peace.

But there are as many forms and types of peace among individuals and nations as there are causes of violence and war. Peace is a remedial rather than an absolute goal; it is the outcome of conflicts and is established in order to prevent other foreseeable conflicts. There is no such thing as total peace, but there is such a thing as total war and total annihilation of rights. Totality, which is inhuman, belongs to fascism, not to us.

Politics does its work of circumventing violence or of discounting the results of violence when conflicts are sharp not when good intentions are eloquent. For this a broad use of symbols and ceremonials is required. Knowledge of politics is knowledge of precise relationships: the relationships between the instruments of government, the men who operate them and the people who bear the brunt of the operating—the relationship between symbols, the caretakers of symbols and the symbolized. Knowledge of politics, as Dante knew, is knowledge of perspectives and proportions which, when observed, sustain society, and when violated, wreck it.

Politics, no matter how organized, is always representative and fiduciary. This means that under every form of politics a few tread a stage which, to be visually effective, has to be a great deal smaller than the arena it faces. The relationship between the players on the stage and the masses in the arena can be of infinite variety, but there are certain laws and perspectives in politics that none of its forms can presume to violate. Of these laws two can be said to be the most important: in politics the few always act for the many; and strict adherence to well-established rules is required to give meaning to the occasional actions of the many.

The driving power that keeps a democracy going is always the hand of the voter who pulls a lever or marks a ballot in an election booth. Yet the hand of the voter is helpless unless a highly complex structure is so tuned as to make the voter's action pertinent and meaningful. Similarly, although the final power in war is the soldier's, whether he releases an atomic bomb or a bow, individual bravery is wasted unless discipline and leadership are there to give it a place in a purposeful plan.

It is through the instruments of politics that the people recognize themselves. They find in these instruments their organs of communication and expression, the manifestation of their purposes and interests. And just as the people are helpless without political tools, so the efficiency of the tools themselves is dependent upon the people's capacity for using them and ultimately paying for them. Dictators are inclined to forget this, as are well-intentioned reformers and planners of ever-normal peace structures. For the life and the fortunes of the people are the ultimate securities that guarantee the gambles both of politics and of war.

The instruments of politics can go a long way toward stimulating or dulling the interests, the needs and the curiosities of the people. The people may try to visualize what is beyond the range of their sight; yet the final usefulness of these telescopes depends upon the capacity of the human eye.

Through politics the bonds imposed on us by the accidental, episodic elements of our work may be loosened or tightened. We can gain an opportunity to emerge from the strictures of our routine of work, to establish other associations and to exert some measure of control over our lives; we can gain an extra reward for our work, or be nailed to it; we can cash our freedom or we are robbed of it.

The kind of work we do is largely the result of chance —chance of birth or of inclination or of connections. The choice of the place and the way we live within the measure of our means is equally the result of chance. So to a large extent are our opinions. And because the element of chance in what we do is so great, and because our future is so unpredictable, we strive through political association to reach a firmer possession of ourselves.

If we are linked to other men, to our party, to our nation, by a common expectation, by a wish for certain happenings, and if we do something to bring about these happenings, then we do better work at our benches and at our desks. But if the political organization to which we belong is patterned on that of our work, our horizon is not much broadened. If Paul is a cobbler, he gains little power by being regarded politically as a cobbler. This is what the proponents of labor parties are inclined to forget. Labor parties can play an essential role in a democracy if they train the workers to look at the world without the blinders of craft or class interest; but they can also solidify the marginal position of the workers.

What men ask of politics is that it give them a firmer grasp on their work and on their lives and at the same time allow them to emerge from the strictures of both, so that they may partially overcome the factor of chance and gain a larger view, exert a more direct influence on a larger world.

Politics is a constant second chance. Men are happy when they are reconciled to what they do and have a chance of doing something else. They are happy when they share in some broader experience than the one they are involved in. That is why political freedom is such an essential element of happiness, particularly since the other-worldliness of religion has lost its appeal as a "something else" for large masses of men. Interest and participation in politics is the something else that men need to feel within their reach in order to be reconciled to what they do and do it well.

There is always a definite and measurable proportion between the people's condition of life and work and the compensation, the something else, that politics can offer. When this proportion is violated, when the compensation is of such a nature as to stifle the imagination of the people or soil it with morbid dreams, then there comes an inevitable reckoning and the people are the ones to pay.

The proportion between conditions of work and political compensations is upset when the political institutions, instead of offering substitutes for war and revolution, are too frequently exposed to them. War inevitably jeopardizes and denounces as superfluous or harmful those instruments which have not succeeded in preventing war. This is true when a defeated people sees that its political institutions have proved unfit to protect them. It is true also for a victorious people if the ensuing peace is shaky and the people are too often called upon to honor the commitments of their leaders with the sacrifice of their lives. War is the final test of institutions, but if the tests are too frequent no political institution is worth its price. The nature of politics is representative but if the represented have too frequently to vouch for the political system with their physical persons, then politics does not pay. Today there are large masses of men all over the world who feel that politics, any kind of politics, does not pay.

Through politics the ties that bind men to their work and to the community may be either strengthened or weakened, and thus the course of the community is set. The art of politics is the art of conducting the community by maneuvering these ties. But there are definite limits to their flexibility, to the amount of pressure they can take. It is not a field open to sweeps of imagination or theoretical vagaries; it is limited, restricted and measurable.

There is a limit to what politics can do in any organized community, national or international, however managed. It can certainly be used for the relief of human misery. It can give not only something else but something better— a betterment of actual and present suffering. But we cannot ask politics to do what even religion could not do: to give men eternal peace or eternal happiness.

The institutions of politics are the tools through which the community may find its direction and move toward it. The direction is determined partly by the demands of economics and technology. Partly, it is an answer to these demands and in opposition to them. This is the way one rides a horse or steers a boat, leaning to the right or the left, managing to overcome obstacles when one's strength or skill can cope with them.

But our latter-day conception of politics has been quite different. People have preferred to float rather than move according to purposes, have responded to the pressure of economics by hoping to redouble its impact, have looked to trends of history rather than to human initiative where purposeful effort can operate.

The truth is that we had largely given up politics, disregarded the operational laws of politics, long before the totalitarian revolts came. We thought of it as a subsidiary mechanism of acceleration, used to speed up economic or technological or social revolutions. The coming of revolutions, the announcement of revolutions, had become the greatest evidence of political wisdom. Before the first World War, and particularly between the two wars, a good way of acquiring repute was gleefully to announce coming revolutions and social earthquakes. The world was full of fretful little brothers of the earthquake.

It is meaningless to be yes-men of history, always managing to be on the safe side and playing up to the inevitable, just as it is meaningless to be quixotic dreamers, angry at the world because it refuses to follow our own ideas of perfection. It is as absurd to disregard politics as to charge it with the realization of absolutes. In the whole set of relationships between men and their work, men among themselves, men and their institutions, there is scarcely one point of conflict or of friction where concerted, timely political effort cannot make a dent. The art of politics consists in recognizing these points and acting on them.

In our day new political ties are being bound on the international level, with the United Nations as the central knot. This does not mean that we can expect the UN to develop into a central government of all nations. The political answer to the thick interrelated unity that industrialism and modern technology have imposed on our world is not to superimpose on it the political unity of a universal state. Rather, it is to check the massive leveling pressure of economics and technology with an international political structure that makes safe and healthy the co-existence of various competing systems of political organization. Our one world will be a free world only if the oneness and massiveness of economics is counter-acted by the multiplicity and elasticity of politics.

CHAPTER II

POLITICAL FREEDOM

Freedom is power, man-made power that men release as a by-product of their labor and that gives them in turn a chance to exert some control over the conditions of their lives. It is man-making power, transmitted to men through their rights, a power that sustains their efforts, makes persons of them, puts them in condition to do their work well and to give back to society, sharpened and refurbished, the power they have absorbed.

The producer-consumer of this power is the individual, but its distribution is social. Rights are the constantly growing driving energies of the world men make, just as the forces of nature are the reservoir of physical power that men increasingly learn to use.

But we do not get the benefit of the forces of nature simply by exposing ourselves to them. We need dams and generators and transformers to bring nature's energy within reach of the individual and adjust it to his needs. We need commonwealth and laws and party politics and administration, centers of organization that reach the individual, to lend him power, make him work, draw power out of him.

Political freedom is the most efficient organization of

116

this dynamic process. It guarantees the most active and productive interrelation between individual citizens and political organs. There are fundamentals in this dynamism that cannot be violated with impunity, particularly in our time. There are laws relating to the political utilization of freedom that are as valid as those physical laws which must be respected when we use nature's resources for the satisfaction of our needs.

Politics is far from being all chance and reckless gamble or a sheer registration of forces—a ceremonial of violence for some, a carbon copy of economics for others. Politics is the technique of using freedom, and freedom is the best that can be made of politics.

Political freedom is freedom of the commonwealth, in the commonwealth, from the commonwealth. It is freedom of the commonwealth from outside oppression and from the whims of its citizens; in the commonwealth and from the commonwealth on the part of its citizens and their groups. These three constituent elements of political freedom are positively interrelated. Each is a function of the others and can be endangered and finally destroyed by the disappearance or the overextension of the others.

In all its three aspects freedom means a limited range of usable power. It is attained and maintained by keeping the commonwealth at a safe distance from certain extreme points. There is a point where the dependence of the commonwealth on the outside becomes so heavy that the internal political organs have no room for choice or decision. There is a point where the arrogant independence of the commonwealth becomes so unrestrained that the citizens are unable to exert any control over the course of public affairs. That is the point of the runaway state. There is a point where the demands of the commonwealth on its citizens become so all-absorbing and exacting that the citizens are transformed into irresponsible tools, with no opportunity ever to forget politics.

The boundaries of the livable zone where political freedom grows are at varying distances from these extreme points. Within this zone, political freedom means a limited range of power embodied in and guaranteed by responsible men. It is a dynamic relationship between elements all of which are necessary and whose reciprocal proportion is variable. It is not represented by any particular type of political organization. There is no such thing as "free political institutions," institutions on whose capacity to guarantee us political freedom we can safely rely. But some institutions more than others are apt to be used for the preservation and production of political freedom.

Three things are required if political freedom is to be generated to any extent: a political community strong enough to enforce its authority; internal organizations that allow the citizens to formulate alternative programs for the course the commonwealth shall take; and finally it requires that the citizens be left alone enough to have a life of their own, with opportunity to make their own experience, test their own worth and assume their own responsibilities.

A margin of independence from the political community does not mean unrestrained enjoyment of privileges by the individual or the people at large. Neither does it imply ir reiterated assent to membership in the community.

It is a poor and shaky compact that needs to be resealed every day.

At the very root of political freedom there is a fundamental distinction between what belongs to the living individual and what belongs to politics, what belongs to the people and what belongs to the organs of the political commonwealth. The generating and the final enjoyment of the energy that is freedom belong to the individual; the channeling, the control, the transmission of this energy belong to politics. To politics is given the care of the instruments that permit the citizens to see themselves as partners of a commonwealth. The institutions of politics are instruments through which the commonwealth becomes visible to the citizens and the citizens relevant to the commonwealth. Through these instruments the citizens can identify themselves with the commonwealth and also protect themselves from it. The political instruments start going wrong when they do not ever allow the release of the individual, when they become automatic, doing the work for him, pretending to be perfect and eternal.

Political freedom functions when the citizen's attitude and means are such that he can both identify himself with the commonwealth and ransom himself from it. For man, however dependent on his institutions he may be, is also their prime mover and their final beneficiary or victim. And the institutions themselves, however elaborate and tested by history, can never perform the individual's task of generating freedom by doing his work well.

Freedom is an attitude of man toward his work and the subject of his work. Political freedom is an attitude of man toward his commonwealth and its political instruments. In both cases freedom means activity, a measure of independence gained through a measure of obedience. A man is not a good citizen and has no claim to call himself a free man if he lacks the capacity to bring back to himself, to compare, absorb and filter, what he has done to the commonwealth and what the commonwealth has done to him. There can be no political freedom unless men know what they can expect of the commonwealth and what the commonwealth can expect of them.

We have grown accustomed to think that there is no difference between what belongs to the people and what belongs to their institutions. We think that because the institutions are theirs, they belong to the people without limit and without reservation, and that at all times and in all places the people are entitled to do just what they please with them. The result of having conceived the commonwealth as belonging unreservedly to the people has been that in some of the most powerful nations on earth the people came to belong to the commonwealth without any possibility of ransom or escape.

Political institutions are not Leviathans, mechanical monsters running on their own power. They are operated by men of more or less skill, and they run on the power that a far greater number of men release. Their function is to channel and distribute this power, but they have a dynamism of their own that becomes more awesome and far reaching as their scope and complexity increase. The men whose function it is to run the instruments of politics are frequently carried away by the power they are supposed to control. Sometimes we are reassured by seeing men at the helm of institutions. Sometimes we are frightened by the power that men can thus concentrate in their own hands.

But government and politics cannot be proper objects of either love or hatred, of blind reliance or systematic mistrust. Of themselves they are neither our friends nor our enemies, neither our masters nor our servants. They are tools of which we are given the use, as different from us as is the living hand from the wheels and knobs it controls.

The tendency, the way of all regimes, good or bad, efficient or wasteful, is to secure the citizens' assent to their programs and their records. Ratification through solicited assent is arrived at in many different ways, from parades to plebiscites to elections, and in all cases a great effort is made to influence the citizens' reactions. This ratification, this coming to grips between citizens and commonwealth, is so essential that not even the most tyrannical regimes can avoid it.

There are two occasions on which a people comes to grips with its institutions and is thoroughly identified with them: during a war, and on election day. In war, the citizens assume the defense of their institutions and redeem the obligations of their leaders with the hard cash of their sweat and blood. On election day, the people and their institutions—the represented and the representative, the symbolized and the symbols—are brought face to face. On that day, the institutions of which the people have the use really belong to them.

Elections can be the most incongruous and crooked ceremonials, or they can be the real evidence of political freedom in a commonwealth. In an election, the social and economic groups in which men are locked by routine or accident are broken up in such a way that the individual has a chance to see himself in the community and as a maker of the community. At these moments, the people take leave of their immediate past and decide their immediate future by choosing from among a few individuals the men in whom they wish to embody their power. There must always be a choice if the election is to be meaningful, and the choice is of men rather than of programs. At these moments, the power of the people is transmitted in measurable, controllable amounts for a stated length of time, to known and named individuals who become responsible for this power and know that on some later occasion they will have to give an account of their stewardship.

Elections are the collective celebrations of political freedom, the moments when political freedom becomes tangible and measurable. Their influence is decisive provided that there are not too many of them and that they are held, so far as possible, at stated intervals. The people's power becomes real and usable when it is parceled among elected individuals to whom the electorate has transmitted a share of power commensurate with their individual capacity and their tested record.

That each citizen receives with his ballot an equal share of political power does not mean that political freedom requires this power to remain equally divided among the citizens. Neither does it mean that all citizens are supposed to have equal skill in handling political tools. Rather, the actual functioning of political freedom produces equality in the sense that it establishes the equivalence of all man's various occupations and modes of life. Political freedom establishes a common denominator among the citizens and gives to their various modes of working and living an equal dignity. The dignity is testified to when, on election day, the groups in which the citizens happen to be divided are broken up. At that moment, the individual, every individual citizen, becomes the protagonist of political life.

But what is the climax of a dynamic process should not be mistaken for a rule that can be identically and constantly applied. The individual is sovereign in the election booth, but no man can spend his life in an election booth. By establishing a common denominator for all types of men and occupations of men, and so reducing their inequality, political freedom burdens with responsibility the men to whom the political institutions are entrusted. It does not leave the institutions at the mercy of individual or collective whims.

When there is political freedom, then at certain moments, on certain specified predetermined occasions, the people and the institutions are brought together, are briefly identified with one another, each equal to the other. During these moments the individual citizen becomes equal to his institutions, with no superior. But after the moment of equality has been celebrated, the people and their institutions again drift apart. Political freedom depends on this parting quite as much as on the moment of identification. For the people and their institutions are not the same, man is not at all times a political animal, and one of the essential conditions of political freedom is that men, in fact the largest possible number of them, be normally allowed to have only occasional and episodic concern with politics.

Political freedom is a condition of things where the people can see themselves as partners of a political community, have opportunity to work for the community and to enjoy a measure of independence from it. It is a condition of things where the individual share of political work is of such a nature as at times to allow participation in communal affairs, at times indifference to them. It is a condition of men reconciled to their work, doing it well, and knowing how to celebrate the essential equality of human experience, the essential equivalence of all forms of work well done. Political freedom is gained both by work and by evasion of work, is celebrated and enjoyed on certain occasions by every member of the community who wants to assert that he is something more than a worker. Political freedom is Sunday.

There is no political freedom when men are kept from evaluating their efforts in terms of individual return or when they are kept from finding a way to improve the conditions of their lives. Political freedom is the surplus profit of work, and free citizenship is the instrument for the collection of this surplus profit. Citizenship is the chief weapon for doing more and better work. It is based on a dynamic interrelation of citizen and worker. An interrelation of two aspects of man, two modes of human experience, it is the answer to the strictures of economics and the means by which improvement can be brought to the economic lot of man. This dynamic interrelation produces free men.

Free men are whole men, men whom we can recognize by the look in their eyes, the poise of their bearing. They are never equal to one another and never have an identical degree of interest in politics. Yet among free men differences of character and modes of work make for a common denominator, because freedom itself establishes communication among them. A free man is one who cares for the welfare of his commonwealth, who knows how to work with it at times and at other times how to keep away from it.

Political freedom is the most efficient system of political organization, the only one in which the essential function of politics can be realized: that is, to compensate men for what they do and reconcile them to what they do. It is to political societies what beauty is to art: a condition of hard-won and immensely communicative inner equilibrium and inner grace. Just as art gives relevance and meaning to the subject matter through which it expresses itself and whose limitations it accepts, so political freedom gives purpose and happiness to the community that succeeds in working out freedom in its politics. Purpose and happiness are not embodied in the mechanism of institutions, but in free men.

CHAPTER III

THE LEVIATHAN

IN THE COURSE of history the amount of power that a commonwealth has been able to absorb, and that individuals have either held in it or wrested from it, has grown prodigiously. Yet the political experience of man has always been processed, however crudely, according to the same pattern: accrual of power by the commonwealth, within the commonwealth, or away from the commonwealth. Politics has always been run within this triangle. When each of the three parts receives its stimulus and check from the full development of the others, then politics is well run.

We are living at a time when the operation of politics in every part of the world has become so interdependent that the privacy of national political experiments has been sharply curtailed. Yet the primary political problem of our time is essentially the same as that of the men whose civilization we inherited: it is the problem of the balanced development of the three forces. The main difference is that our fathers, acting in smaller and more sheltered areas, enjoyed a far broader margin for error.

But the search for political freedom did not start with the English or French Revolutions or even with Christianity. The pre-Christian commonwealths of the West were disrupted when self-sustaining, self-centered individuals started to ask why they should be tied by political obligations. Christianity, in establishing the difference between what belongs to God and what to Caesar, made the Christian a citizen of two communities at the same time. It gave the individual an opportunity for security and growth by allowing him to be a citizen of an earthly and of a spiritual community and to struggle for power in one against the other or for one inside the other. At the same time he learned how to gain a measure of personal independence from one or the other and frequently from both.

Western civilization has been marked by the struggle of men to make their identification with their commonwealth limited, occasional and subject to ritual and tradition. It has been a story of people who found in the church the power to fight a prince, or rallied around a prince in their struggle against the church, or entrenched themselves in parliaments to challenge a royal court. In more recent times men have learned how to bind themselves to political parties within their states, thus striving for the authority of the commonwealth when in power, and for independence from it when out of power.

It is the nature of political parties to be reproductions of the state, fashioned according to various combinations of interests and different expectations of future events. A political party is a voluntary association of citizens who play at being the state, pretend to be the people, and reproduce among themselves, with the stuff of their every-

day emotions, interests and prejudices, the formal structure
of the constitutional legal order.

Parties are the informal popular counterparts of inevitably remote and abstract constitutional rules. Constitutional rules do not live of themselves in mystical majesty.
They are vitalized when their structure is filled in with
the content of current emotions, interests and prejudices.
In the United States, the Constitutional Convention is
celebrated every four years by the two major political
parties who, with a great display of showmanship and
obedience to time-worn ceremonials, reseal in their own
way the federal compact of the nation.

In a modern democratic society the relationship between
the people and the state is entrusted to political parties.
Men train themselves in these small-scale reproductions
to run the state or to protect themselves from it. A political
party pretends to represent the people, or at least a majority of the people, while actually it includes a comparatively small number of citizens. It speaks for the people
until its claim is tested at the next election, when for one
day large masses of the citizens take upon themselves the
responsibility of being the people. But even when a party
turns out to be a minority, the rule of the game is that it
must act as if it were a potential majority until the next
time those who go to the polls again take on the job of
being the people's voice.

When the party system works, the identification of a
group of citizens with the community and the hold that a
winning group acquires on the public organs are always
tentative and precarious, fixed only for a limited time and
having limited purposes. On the way partisan politics
works, political freedom largely depends, since the dual

allegiance to state and party seems to have replaced that formerly given to prince and church, to Caesar and God.

The working of political parties is based on the political activity of the few and the relative indifference of the many—an indifference that may occasionally turn into a large-scale popular militancy. Political parties actually distribute political power among the citizens in accordance with the citizens' political skill. They keep the general concern simmering and channel the periodic upsurges of political interest. These highly pragmatic reproductions of the state are run more according to the rough and tumble of expediency than the dictates of principle. Their bulk is extraordinarily elastic: they appear almost as fleshy as the nation just before election day, but shrink between elections to a skeleton propped up by ward leaders and part-time bosses. They are always likely to abuse their power unless fear of the politically inactive or moderately active citizens keeps the politicians in check. When a political party assumes in all earnestness to be the state and frees itself from fear of its opponents and of the inactive citizens, then the democratic game is up.

The distance between the people and their commonwealth is guaranteed in democratic societies by the struggle for power of political parties within the state. The old pre-democratic game was played in a fixed setting and with two main protagonists like Church and State or Parliament and King. Our modern democratic game is infinitely more complex in its endless variety. It is also more realistic since, like the modern theatre, it pretends to reproduce real life in its stage settings. The essence of the game is that an alternative leadership and program must always be at hand as a channel for popular revulsion. But in our time as in pre-democratic times the violence of the political struggle is mitigated by the expectation of future gains—in another world for the medieval Christians, at the next election for modern democracies.

This function of maintaining a relationship between commonwealth and people, and preserving distance between them, moderates the heat of political passion and blunts the sharpness of political issues; yet it is far from being welcomed or praised by the official philosophies of democracy. Rather, it is considered a shocking if forgivable consequence of the frailty of human nature, a practical necessity which hampers full realization of democratic ideals. True democracy, it is said, means a constant identification between people and commonwealth, a relentless participation of the citizens—of all of them all of the time—in their political affairs. The elementary facts of political life are the normal political disinterest of the many and the lucrative political activity of the few. But these facts, shunned by our perfectionists, acquire the character of curious and piquant indecency. The result is that the inactive citizens are flattered by the periodic tirades against their persistent inactivity, and the full-time professionals reap large benefits from their unregulated trade.

The perfectionistic conception of politics is the origin of most of our political fallacies, all based on the notion that the relationships between citizens and commonwealth can be firmly set according to an "ideal" ever-normal pattern. This attitude is typically exemplified by the marxist creed which conceives of the political struggle in terms of class conflict between the so-called proletariat and the so-called bourgeoisie. The implication is that one of these classes must ultimately liquidate the other in a political struggle to end all political struggles.

Long before marxism, another and more far-reaching fallacy had poisoned the roots of modern democracy. This fallacy concerned the relationship between the individual, the people and the state, dogmatically proclaiming it an absolute identity: the individual is the people and the people are the state.

More than twenty centuries of effort aimed at establishing stable boundary lines between the people and the commonwealth, in the interest of both, has been endangered by this fallacy. Since the state belongs to the people, the people, it maintains, are in fact the state; and since what is called the people means the generality of the citizens, the citizen is the state. On this trinity of citizen-people-state what pretends to be the democratic dogma of popular sovereignty rests.

The citizen is of the state, he lends to its institutions his passions and interests and even his blood; he lives and works largely because of the state, but *he is not* the state. He is beyond it and above it, but it is not he, nor he it. The great mistake is to say to the citizen: you are the state. It is a corrupting mistake, an injustice both to the individual and the people as a whole. Inevitably the moment will come when some individual or group will step forward and proclaim: I am the state. By being enthroned as the state, the people lose either the sense or the protection of their institutions—and ultimately both. Leviathan is far shrewder than Caliban.

For the people, the state is the ultimate object of obedience and the final testing ground of independence, a constant link with their past that gives relevance to their lives and their work. The people lend their reality to the state, they hold it, they keep it up, but they are not it and they do not own it. In fact, there is no such thing as ownership of a state, great or small, no matter whether the would-be owner is a king or the whole of the people. There are persons calling themselves democrats who, in order to obviate the ownership of the state by one man, would have that ownership shared by every living man in the commonwealth. When they do this they multiply the fallacy they pretend to denounce.

When men are told, "You are the state, the state is you and belongs to you," they are burdened with an impossible task. Modern political communities are too large, too complex and too unpredictable in their course, for the individual to feel secure in his understanding of the whole process in which he is involved.

Given the sense that he is the state, with the whole of it his province, the citizen is lost or baffled. There are no political instruments that can redress the disproportion between the realm of his immediate experience and the wide social scene that he is supposed to encompass with his understanding and animate with his decisions. What is called the sovereign democratic state bewilders and frustrates his intelligence, stirs his appetites, irks his nerves and leaves his heart empty.

In actuality, while so-called democratic theory is predicated on total and constant identification between people, individual and state, democracy has prospered only where such identity was loosely held. Such is the case in England, where the rigidity of the democratic dogma is tempered by the remnants of monarchy and feudalism; and it is the case in the United States where the people's participation in political affairs is distracted—sometimes past the point of safety—by an all-absorbing concern with business.

The people have degrees of identification with the state and with the instruments of politics that make the state comprehensible to them, degrees that range from a minimum to almost total identification when the state is engaged in a great war. War means total and therefore unfree politics, total absorption of the people in the state. In time of war and revolution the people have nothing else to do, no personal business other than that of belonging to the community and sharing its destiny. In time of peace we have instead of total politics, limited politics, loose or elastic politics.

Peace is marked by the fact that men acquire something else to do, their own small or big businesses, their own small or big schemes. We have normal peacetime politics then, ordinary politics where men start playing their own partisan games with a view to resolving their conflicts by means other than armed warfare and total absorption in the state. They can even afford not to care.

By constantly repeating to individuals and to the people as a whole that they are the state, the democratic dogma has offered a wartime creed as a justification for an order of things that is supposed to lead to everlasting peace. By hammering away that the individual is the state, that the people are the state and that citizens, people and state form a unity, individuals and groups have, in some countries, been brought so close to the state that the groups have

melted and the steel-like structure of the totalitarian state
has emerged.

The mistaken notion of freedom is at the core of this
concept of popular sovereignty. Its assumption is that the
political community, the state, being subject to no one, is
free, and that the individual and the people can reach freedom by becoming more and more identified with their
state.

One of the most characteristic trends of our time is the
belief that the people can gain security and happiness
by multiplying their dependence on political and economic institutions. This is the essence of marxism, which
pretends to solve economic difficulties by coupling national sovereignty with national monopoly. There are
even those in our day who think that the way out of the
difficulties that constantly arise inside and outside the state
is to attain the superstate, the universal state. The trend
of mind is unmistakable: to reach a size where evil does
not work because in bigness lies salvation.

The identification of the people with the state, the absorption of the people and of their functions by the state,
has been called democracy. When it becomes the property
of all the people within its borders, the state can do no
wrong and the people become free. There are many who
still call this democracy. Those who long for lawlessness
call it freedom, but when the totalitarian state comes to
satisfy their wishes they fill the air with their offended
cries—particularly if they happen to be on the losing side.

As a form of order rather than lawlessness, democracy
is the mature and humane discipline of men who know

how to run themselves well, how to respect their own rights and the requirements of their institutions, how to obey those institutions, to run them and to be independent of them. But the people's power over themselves has been interpreted as power to do what they pleased with themselves. It was thought that this power was total and boundless and could be directly exerted by the people over their institutions, enabling them even to throw away their institutions if they pleased. If democracy is such a thing, it is but a name for chaos.

Surely the strength of modern democracy must be extraordinarily great if it could survive and flourish in spite of the fallacies that poisoned the start of its career on the European continent. What is the result of a high-tension equilibrium, a hard-won and intermittently celebrated identification between citizen, people and commonwealth, was regarded by the radical or Rousseau school of thinking as a permanent, ever-working and ever-workable relationship. A more or less sweeping interpretation of the total process and its final outcome was made into a pattern for its daily routine, twenty-four hours a day.

It is true that the reality of the state is the people and that the reality of the people is man and that all organs of social action and perception are scaled according to the needs of man. It is also true that the secret and the test of the process is the individual's capacity to grow as a particle of the people and to find his place in the community. But all this withers, breaks down, when we start assuming that the process is uniform and inevitable, that the identification between individual and commonwealth is permanent and unfailing. For man is not the state but the measure and test of the state.

Democracy is not at fault; the fault lies in the interpretation of it as a regime within which the people can build or tear down their institutions according to their whims— not least that most fatal of all whims, the attempt to gain freedom by embodying the sovereignty of the state. It is not the idea of national or state sovereignty which is at fault, if this means enjoyment by the commonwealth of a large margin of independence from outside interference. Indeed, such enjoyment is an essential element of political freedom. Unless the state has some margin for action and for error, there is little hope of freedom for the individual. But individual freedom has no chance at all if the sovereignty that the state attains is boundless and unchecked.

The principle of popular sovereignty itself is not at fault if what it means is that the sovereignty of the state is guaranteed and checked by the people, by their limited capacity and willingness to pay. Popular sovereignty should mean a check on those who man the institutions of government, not a blank endorsement of their ruthlessness. It should mean a system of accounting that prevents the rulers, no matter how appointed, from assuming commitments beyond the people's capacity to pay.

When interpreted as boundless power, popular sovereignty leaves the people to bear the brunt of what the men who manipulate their institutions have made them do. Demagogic rulers unfailingly leave the people to foot the bill when their military or political adventures end in disaster. The institutions they have wrecked appear but weird assemblages of habits and rules. When institutions crumble, those who manned them usually manage to get away—by dying, if they have no other recourse, or by lying low, waiting for the moment when they can emerge as technicians or experts. The people, however, pay. The institutions are a shambles and their manipulators are in hiding—but the people remain. They pay, but their payment cannot bring relief to them or settle the debts they have incurred. What the crumbling of institutions does to the people cannot be visualized or measured, because with their fall the institutions carry along all instruments of visualization and measurement.

We have seen in our own time horrible examples of what happens to sovereign peoples who, lured by demagogues, have been deluded into thinking they could reach freedom and power by giving all of themselves to their state. We have seen some of the most civilized peoples of Europe coming closer and closer to the organs of their state, making idols of what are instruments of work, giving all their labor and emotion and allegiance to the man whom they considered the embodiment of their state. The closer they came, the more thoroughly and inescapably they were trapped, until they had to give all of their blood and all of their soul. But it was never enough.

We have seen great peoples, great nations, debauched beyond recognition, sacking the patrimony of their rights. When the end came, nothing was left but a disjointed people, a people without institutions, a rabble of men and women who had no chance of knowing what they had done or what they wanted or what they needed. By giving themselves to their institutions without reserve, the people wrecked their institutions and themselves. In the end they lost the protection of their institutions and lost themselves. "Everything in the state, nothing outside the state, nothing against the state," they were told. But this is a prescription of death both for the state and the people. The people—all the people in certain nations—came too close to the great condensers and transformers of power.

In the impact they were burned and their power houses collapsed.

There is constant tendency toward rupture and waste of power on each side of the triangle of forces that makes up the dynamism of political freedom. It shows itself when national independence becomes boundless, irresponsible sovereignty; or when the internal struggle for power becomes a ruthless conflict of ideologies and interests, each bent on outlawing the other; or finally when the independence of individuals and groups from the political commonwealth becomes an irresponsible scramble of whims. Wherever it occurs, the rupture is due to the fact that that particular side of the triangle has tried to expand boundlessly.

Democracy is the name for a political order that gives to the generality of people the fullest enjoyment of the rights that the past has left them, and to each single citizen the best possible compensation for his work, the best possible chance to do his work well. It is not the name for a political order that debauches the people by letting them believe they are holding or can ever hold the boundless suicidal lawlessness of the sovereign state.

Popular sovereignty should never mean a system under which the people are constantly called upon to make unlimited payment for the misdeeds of their leaders. Rather, it should mean limited sovereignty, because its power is guaranteed by the citizens, whose capacity for payment is limited. It should mean an order of things that gives to the individual components of a society the greatest possible benefit of association at the lowest possible cost.

The state is the particular social institution that faces the future, the unforeseeable events, trying to link these to previously laid plans and purposes. It is the spot where ultimately the threads of social and individual action are pooled and woven together, the spot permanently dedicated to the finishing of unfinished business. There is no spot more delicate, none more artificial by reason of the nature of the tools, none with greater effect upon that deepest reality, the people. In a well-run society, the state is the people's state, the people's trust, managed by accountable trustees. It is a place of business, of highly vital business, not an amusement park. Nor is it a shrine where miracles may be commanded at will.

A point of saturation has been reached where the old delusions and errors are no longer bearable. There are unmistakable demands and unmistakable facts before us. The old fallacies about democracy and popular sovereignty are now being championed by parties that want to do away with democracy and with the people's participation in their own affairs. At the same time, all over the world, the people have paid an exorbitant penalty for old and new misconceptions—and in more than one country they know it. There are new organs in existence that can correct the old errors. There are new facts in politics, new types and knots of power, which must be reckoned with if we are to establish the right relationship between institutions and people, governments and living men.

CHAPTER IV

THE NEW POLITICS

O<small>UT</small> of this world civil war there is emerging a new political order that does not easily accommodate itself to our traditional patterns of political thinking. But if we succeed in adjusting our ideas to this new order, we can perhaps accelerate the process of its ripening.

During these difficult war and postwar years we have been tossed from dismay to dejection to still greater dismay. We came to realize during wartime that governments in exile or committees of national liberation had a doubtful claim to represent their people and that it was up to the people, when freed, to give themselves a "government of their own choosing." After peace came, we had to acknowledge the fact that some liberated nations were prevented from or did not know how to use the instruments of popular representation. And even where elections were, as it was said, "unfettered," we could see that it was often questionable whether governments "of the people's choosing" were genuinely representative of the electorate.

Hedged about by uncomfortable facts, we cling to our time-worn conceptions of rights and freedom and popular sovereignty or keep relying on words and taking them at their face value. Thus we are willing to accept as a political party any organization that calls itself one, even when it is not the fifth but the first vanguard column of an invading foreign power. Or else, when we are finally alarmed by the deceitful parties, we think that by denying them legal existence we can go a long way toward eradicating their causes.

We register protests against the ruthlessness that the communist parties exhibit when they thrive under the shadow of the Red Army, and we equally protest the impudent mimicry of democracy that the communists indulge in wherever the absence of the Red Army forces them to play democracy's game. We make loud outcries whenever we realize that the various communist national parties are weapons of Russia's power, and we are stunned whenever we see how undemocratically undemocratic forces are prone to act.

One moment we pay tribute to the principle of election, as the medium through which every nation can give itself the order it pleases; another moment we assert the supreme desirability of an all-embracing universal state to whose rule every nation should be subordinate. Merrily we proclaim the supreme value of sovereignty (provided it is popular), and then that of man (provided it is common). Finally, we think we can outlaw both militarism and war by establishing world government, because rebellions against this government are to be fought not by soldiers, but by policemen.

Over and over again we hear the complaint that ideological content was lacking in our war, and now we are alarmed because, having won the war, we are in danger of "losing the peace." We were thoroughly dismayed when it became clear at the end of the hostilities that the world civil war was still going on. We complain that just when the war has again become political, we find ourselves with few or inadequate political weapons.

While the military war was being fought, the most notable achievements of political warfare have been two: the recognition that our world is one world, and the formulation of the four freedoms. Yet the one world that was discovered bore little resemblance to our round world where midnight at one point is noon somewhere else. It was a flat one world that was discovered, meant to be swept from one end to the other by the same forces of good fellowship. And the enthusiasm for the discovery was so great that it prevented the consideration of the kind of oneness that we, the inhabitants of the world, were most likely to enjoy.

The same shallowness marked the conception of the four freedoms, whose range of practical validity was defined as "everywhere in the world." Moreover, the accent was never put on the one point where it belongs: that each of the four freedoms, if cultivated for its own sake, is destined to lead men straight into slavery. Obsession with freedom from want can lead us into communism, just as the urge to be free from fear can bring us to fascism. It is the same process that derives irresponsible thinking from freedom of thought, and loss of the sense of the divine from freedom of worship. For the major ills of our time seem to come from the one-sided, overstretched attempt to pursue a single one of the four freedoms.

What is essential is not the full enjoyment of any one of the four "everywhere in the world," but the balanced interfusion of all four at definite spots in the world— indeed, at the largest possible number of spots in the world. Where this happens, even the overextension of one of the four freedoms at the expense of the others turns out to be temporary and tolerable.

Yet these two principles, the oneness of the world and the four freedoms, come close to the core of the real novelty that has been emerging from the war and from the peace.

The novelty is not one of ideology, nor does it lie in the realm of political thinking or even of political institutions. It is not contained in any manifesto or quotable doctrine. It found its first form in statutes drafted by lawyers with the support of statisticians and foreign office specialists. It showed itself through various devices with various names: Lend-Lease, UNRRA, the Marshall Plan. No one of these structures created under the spur of emergency was designed to cover more than a certain span of time and circumstance. Wherever the attempt was made to convert the underlying principles into a doctrine, we ran into dangerous, misty vagueness, as in the case of the Truman Doctrine.

Yet the trend is unmistakable. It is concerned primarily with what comes before politics, it aims at giving a certain protection to that fundamental reality, the human stuff that political institutions are made of. What is great and new in the politics of our time has little to do with the supremacy of one commonwealth or type of commonwealth; it has no connection with the imperialistic drives of the communist or the capitalist internationals. It does not set itself to break new ground in politics but rather to consolidate the terrain on which political structures, both old and new, may become strongly rooted and grow.

Vague as the conception of one world and the four freedoms was, it marked the new trend. The war itself revealed the inescapable need for a degree of welfare and security everywhere. It became clear that a minimum of economic and political well-being for all men is a matter of inter-human and international concern, for every political order is made up of people, and the elementary needs of the people have priority over the vagaries of politics. Actually the new politics is the politics of the obvious, based on the slowly awakening sense of the sacredness of the obvious.

This trend has gone forward, irrepressibly, through both the military and the political phases of the world civil war. Victory itself, the hard-won people's victory, was nothing but an obligation that political action and political thinking must still redeem.

This trend long antedates the war and goes far deeper than all the motives and political ideologies that have been attributed to the war. It is irrepressible in spite of the attempts that politicians made to interpret it or capture it. It has been ushered into the world at the time when industrialism has started to energize and yet to endanger our civilization.

Industrialism has established an increasing relationship and interdependence among the various reservoirs of experience and skill. Now it has happened that the peoples who until now have had no chance want to start building their own reservoirs, because the formulae for building them have become as available as they are alluring.

Industrialism has pushed into the foreground those primary conditions of life and work that underlie the structure of every commonwealth, great and small, powerful or weak, and that are of equal necessity to all. These conditions involve the very existence of every individual everywhere. For men everywhere have been reached by industrialism, uprooted from their communities, thrown into new associations and forced to contribute their work.

Industrial civilization denounced the setting and the background of all the various organized centers of political activity. By putting tools into the hands of men of backward nations, it gave them a chance to have rights. At the same time it sapped the foundations of national security and independence by establishing at the margin of the most civilized communities large masses of uprooted men. Because the marginal value of freedom determines its course, internal peace was threatened everywhere. Because the marginal value of sovereignty represented by the weakest or poorest nations debases the value of sovereignty, international peace was threatened everywhere.

Communism is the main form that this double threat has taken, because communism is the main attempt to exploit these two major ruptures of our civilization. Communism thrives wherever the marginal condition of the workers is most painful and the misery and ignorance of the people most abject. It tries to harness these elements in an international political movement, in order to form a universal state that should, in time, wither away. The aim of communism is to produce a political revolution that will forever eradicate politics in our world.

Communism, unlike fascism, is not a mad, suicidal attempt to secede from our civilization. Its reasoning is the extreme, vicious conclusion of the already vitiated elements of our thinking; its attempt to short-cut the individual and make freedom meaningless is based on a one-sided, halfway interpretation of industrialism; and, like certain schools of democratic thinking, it is founded on the belief that economic forces will find an automatic, self-adjusting course, once certain obstacles are removed. Both the conditions that make for communism and the communist way of thinking are democracy's undivided responsibility.

Our relationship with this far-flung projection of our errors is too intimate ever to be settled by war. It is at the same time highly useful to us, because communism has the power to become the vital stimulant we need to shake from their obsolescence our patterns of political thinking and political action. In fact, the communist offensive upon our modes of living and of thinking is already determining the conditions and the organs by which it can be offset.

Some of these organs are already in operation. They are by no means national organs and they are only to a limited extent political. They have to do with food, with currencies, with regulation of exports and imports—in fact, with many of the essentials of life.

It is an apparently slow, complex grinding process. From time to time it may attract attention—as, for instance, at a great international conference when a plan for international co-operation is to be drafted. But ordinarily it is shy of publicity and remarkably shy of politics—at least of that inconclusive politics that pervades the platforms where international dissents are dramatized.

Significantly enough, these aimless, old-fashioned debates are particularly cherished by Soviet Russia, while the functional bodies, toiling with hard facts and trying to accomplish something, are consistently shunned or mistrusted. Communism has no sympathy with attempts to deal with the pre-political causes of political controversies. It has no patience with prophylactic methods but tries to bring every disease to the point where it will need surgical intervention.

Through Soviet Russia and its satellites, communism is firmly entrenched in the United Nations and neglects no opportunity to use the platform it affords. But the UN is a peculiar organization, useful to communism and at the same time utterly uncongenial to it. It speaks the language of democracy, it is built according to democratic principles and perspectives; its tools—votes, majority rule, representation, etc.—are the tools of democratic procedure. Within the UN the communists can declaim and intrigue, at its periphery they can agitate and subvert. Yet the United Nations that the communists use because of the publicity it affords also hampers their intriguing and subverting because of the light it throws on them.

Within the United Nations communism is increasingly cornered. It cannot walk out because that platform is too useful, but it does not want to work for the elimination of the real causes of international disturbance. It can only make politics and more politics, denouncing itself for what it is: a negative force, tremendously irritating, and tremendously useful for the stimulation of positive action and positive thinking.

Meanwhile, the functional and regional, pre-political work goes on within the UN and outside it. New principles are gradually coming to be recognized as supreme laws of the international community. These principles have to do with basic elementary things, like rates of employment and consumption and production—sometimes even with such elementary and presumably laughable things as calories.

Peacetime full employment is slowly becoming the test of a new legitimacy. It is a heavily conditioned legitimacy that leaves little room for the mad sweep of authoritarian ideologies or unchecked sovereignty; for no government, however powerful, is actually able to guarantee peacetime full employment without the co-operation of its citizens and the assistance of the outside world.

Increasingly, the right to work acquires the dignity of a universal, pre-political right—pre-political because it is coming to be recognized as the unquestionable foundation of whatever legal and political order men can give themselves. It holds the same position that the right of property held when it was considered the fundamental principle that every political order was founded upon. And nothing could be more proper than this shift of emphasis from property to work, since work has become the essential power of our civilization—a power that every individual releases, that conditions the enjoyment of all other rights and that, if it is not to degenerate into slavery, presupposes the full operation of all other rights.

It is becoming clear that unless the largest possible number of men is in a condition to consume and produce, the wealth and power of great nations are precarious and ephemeral things. This simple truth is increasingly driven home to all men every day and, if in a piecemeal, groping way, is being acted upon. It is reflected in those international functional organs dealing with the essential needs of men, that are activated whenever human needs become particularly acute and communist attempts to exploit them particularly vicious.

This work is constantly exposed to ideological disturbances, as well as to attempts to engineer legal mechanisms that are supposed forever to outlaw needs and suffering, politics and freedom. It is just as well that it should remain in the background a while longer, enmeshed in its unglamorous technicalities. While the work proceeds, it is all to the good that communism goes on shrieking and subverting, fighting democracy and mimicking democracy. For with its agitations communism not only peremptorily indicates the fields where the work is most urgent, but at the same time denounces itself as a way of looking at life and conceiving politics which is as debasing as it is outdated.

There are people who think they know how to reckon with the conditions of modern technology dramatized by the new instruments of warfare. They think that world political unity would re-enforce the unity that technology has imposed on us. Just as there have always been people who, stirred by political abuses, thought that the abolition of political parties was the only safeguard of a stable democratic order, so there are many today who, because sovereignty has brought much evil, see the abolition of national sovereignty as the only guarantee of international peace. Such people have a poor understanding of the function of politics and an even poorer understanding of freedom.

Politics is not a carbon copy of economics, embroidered with ideological trimmings and smeared by the heavy thumbs of its practitioners. Its function is to bring the data of economics and technology within the range of human sight and control. Half of the function of politics is to register facts; the other half is to act upon them.

The chief fact that politics in our time must register is the economic integration of the world. The way to act on this is not to abolish national sovereignties but to bring them within those conditions and limitations that make every freedom effective. The function of politics in our day is not to build a house where all men would feel lost, but to co-ordinate the services which are needed to improve the conditions of life in the places where men live. The hope of our world is not in the establishment of a universal system of rights entrusted to a sovereign super-state, but in the gradual synchronization of the various systems of rights.

For in our time there are basic elements common to every system of rights whose synchronization is not only possible but imperative. The most fundamental of these common elements is the condition of the individual: wherever he lives, he is a measurable unit of production and consumption who has an absolute need to extricate himself from the ever-present worry about production and consumption.

There is a trend toward the synchronization of the systems of rights. Functions and activities that are international in scope are becoming the object of a measure of international control. This is not a result of peace but a condition of peace. The regulation of currencies, the international discipline of trade, the discipline of migrations, the control of international credit and communication, all these are elementary conditions of peace. They are being concentrated upon by international organizations, functional in character, regional or universal in operation.

Since the industrial revolution began, no nation has been really free, but simply loose, exposed and fearful. The more firmly the pre-political conditions of life are established, the more secure and independent the political structure of any nation can be.

The better the international functional organs work, the more the sovereign state can become responsible to its own people for their welfare and to the rest of the world for the welfare of its own people. Sovereignty becomes an essential element of the dynamism of freedom once it is ballasted by this double obligation. This will never create identity of standards all over the world but, like the dynamism of rights, will stimulate the growth of different orders and establish common denominators among them. Like all the products of the dynamism of rights, the United Nations is meant to establish a minimum cost for independence and association, a high price for disturbance and secession.

Awareness of the right to work as a universal prepolitical right means recognition of every community's need for an order of things that will allow its citizens, individually and in association, to cope with the hazards of their labor. The right to work can be organized differently in the various communities once machineries are set in motion to establish international minimum standards or collective well-being. From then on, it will be in the interest of peace that every nation be independent and sovereign, because sovereignty will have a purpose and a check. Every nation will produce as much freedom as it can, and its citizens will gain or strengthen as many rights as they are worth.

Once the basic pre-political activities are organized through adequate functional organs, the game of international politics can only serve to strengthen this order. Control of the pre-political framework then becomes the stake of politics. This may result in occasional threats to peace, but the common framework linking all peoples and nations both defines and limits the scope of possible conflicts. Should total war break out again, everything would be lost for all.

The more effectively the pre-political organizations operate, the greater the wedge that will be driven between the individual and the state. The state can never again assert that the individual belongs to it, when it is established that the individual does not receive all his means of working and living from the state. And the people will never again claim that the state belongs to them and that they can do with it what they please, when it becomes clear that the state is only a trustee, a responsible holder of a common wealth, common to all and owned by no one. Thus the conquest of the state by internal political forces, the playing of internal politics, will lose a great deal of its overbearing value.

The clearest example of the new politics is in the responsibility the American nation has assumed for the economic restoration of the world. This is the insurance premium that American power pays for its survival, while the opponents of America can do little but foment troubles in the countries that America assists. On one side, America's opponents harp on "democracy," and offer nothing but a bloody caricature of its most outworn sloganized dogmas; on the other, America is laboriously discovering how to guarantee the independence of foreign people, how to create conditions that will enable other nations to share with America the responsibilities of reconstruction and power, and become independent of America.

The essence of the new politics is that power in all its forms, irrespective of its magnitude, is increasingly ballasted by effective responsibilities. The greater the power, the greater the responsibility, and the greater the need of shouldering these responsibilities, if power is to endure. Politics becomes compensated and limited, not boundless.

Dictatorial fullness of political power is the mark of regimes that are at the same time obsolete and doomed.

The international organization of politics and the synchronization of the systems of rights require a wide range of difference both in the power and in the internal political institutions of the various countries. The principle of the equality of nations is something more than a sing-song of international diplomacy. Rather, the respect of this principle is an essential condition for the participation in international life of nations able to rule themselves and to assume their share of international responsibility. This responsibility, which is commensurate to the power of each nation, implies rights and duties of which no nation can be deprived. In international affairs, as in every other field, the first condition for the equalizing function of rights is the inequality among the bearers of rights.

We need great and small states in our world, facing in different ways the similar problems of our times. In the same way, the essential similarity of circumstances imposed by the mechanical mode of labor everywhere can be dealt with only if different methods of political organization apply themselves to the same tasks.

These differences of political criteria are not determined by the whims of ideologies, nor are they to be welcomed simply for the sake of their differences. They are for the most part determined by the manifold interpretations that were given to the economic and political course of industrial civilization. It is proper that different regimes cohabit within the same structure, because each in its own way represents a particular blend of prevailing truths and fallacies. It is proper that they all exist to check and consume one another.

The internal political systems of the nations within the UN range from the various types of democracy in the Anglo-Saxon countries to the collectivism of Soviet Russia. There is no reason why the democracies should be spared so uncomfortable a neighbor, since they themselves were largely responsible for communism. Given the conditions of our times, it is just as essential that Soviet Russia set and preserve the pattern of active productive socialism as that the American nation set and preserve the pattern of internal economic competition. There is an actual division of labor in our world that distributes among the various nations the risks of industrial progress.

The United Nations can become strong only through the constant explosion of the conflicts inherent in our civilization. The power that keeps the international machinery going is the regulated combustion of all those forces which, if left unchecked, would lead to the blast of war.

In our times there are four major prerequisites of international political order, four conditions that the various members of the international community may meet in different degree but which must be present in the community as a whole. The first is active international competition for the control of the agencies that administer the pre-political international functions. The second is the existence of independent governments capable of doing what is in their power to do and differing from each other in type and range of power. The third is the existence of private property, which means something limited and physical to which the citizen can hold, which is his responsibility and gives him a measure of himself. The fourth is the availability of substitutes for property in the form of social security and assistance, in order that the citizen may enjoy a measure of independence from the fluctuations of his economy.

It is fortunate that these four conditions are unevenly met by the nations of the world. The dynamic equilibrium of the international community does not need to be reflected by an identical political equilibrium in each of its component parts.

The unity that the world may hope to achieve is not one imposed by uniformity of political ideology or economic discipline. Rather it must spring from below, from those pre-political functional structures which satisfy needs that no single state by itself can cope with. At the same time, the growth of this unity, the articulation of this oneness, must be interpreted and guided so that unity may be achieved not for its own sake and at any cost, but as an instrument of freedom, giving increased range and power to the dynamism of freedom. The function of interpreting and guiding belongs to us who believe in freedom and work for it. From our communist competitors we can expect only challenges and tests of our strength.

In such agencies of the United Nations as the Economic and Social Councils and the Committee of Human Rights we have and will increasingly have clearing-houses where the functioning of rights within the various national communities is compared and graded according to basic common denominators. The violations of fundamental human freedoms and of the basic conditions of human well-being cannot be hidden either by censorship or by propaganda.

The international community may not be in a condition to redress them, but they become known, denounced, and are neither forgiven nor forgotten.

It is this grading and comparing of rights according to common denominators that brings about their synchronization. But synchronization does not mean identity or equivalence. At no stage does the dynamism of rights produce or presuppose mathematical equality or equivalence of results. Rather, it produces floors and ceilings between which inequalities and differences may be gradually reduced.

A free world is a city of many mansions. There are also cottages and slums. But slums are rundown cottages, and mansions and their dwellers must have a chance to repair or rebuild them, if the city is to be safe.

There is a hierarchy among the various types of political and social organizations. There are nations that have been wise over a period of centuries in caring for their own rights. There are nations that for ages have had a hand-to-mouth relationship with freedom, and there are nations whose citizens are so unfortunate as to be completely deprived of the profits of their labor and have no chance ever to emerge from it. There is room for many types of nations in our world, provided there is an underlying functional unity which furnishes a floor of minimum subsistence and decency beneath which no people may be allowed to fall.

With firm pride we can say that democracy, when it is not poisoned by the heresies that inevitably lead to totalitarianism, when it is continually checked in the individual and by the individual, is the highest and most efficient form of government that has been arrived at up to our day. On certain occasions its citizens can emerge from the drudgery of their work and the casualness of their associations. At certain moments they have opportunity to check a definite span of their experience, to become reconciled to it and to plan some improvement in it. In a truly representative order there are moments when freedom becomes visible and tangible in the quiet, poised, self-reliant power of its citizens.

This is democracy: an order of things where the course of public affairs is constantly keyed to the needs, the wishes, the limited capacities of the people, and where the people key their lives and work to the demands of public affairs. The nations that enjoy this order do not need to have it imposed by self-appointed custodians, nor do they need to memorize democracy by constantly mouthing the word democracy. They are democracy.

The new politics that is emerging is played on a world-wide scale because there are world-wide needs and functions that industrial civilization has revealed and that we must both regulate and use. It is politics played against a common background, with a common stake, by different nations having different orders and motives. It is politics with a subject matter, politics played for power but not for sheer power, because power now can find its function in the discharge of specific responsibilities. There is room in this political game for any form of regime that is willing to accept differences in types of government and unity of purpose. But the one form that is the beacon for all the others and that deliberately mediates their differences is the democracy of the great nations of the West. Each of the other forms of government is supposed to make good in the areas it presumes to rule. But representative democracy is the only one that sets and keeps the standards of national and international government. Should it lose its hold on the areas of the world where it is sovereign, the whole new system of politics would break down.

The United Nations, which is the core of the new system, is the first evidence that politics is acquiring a new dimension. At the same time, it allows the gradual liquidation of the old politics. Within the new dimension, strange, unconventional things are happening, links are being strengthened among sovereign and equal nations, while the functional organs whittle down sovereignty and gradually correct the inequalities of power and resources among nations.

The United Nations can live up to its function provided it does not develop into a government, but gradually forces on all governments common standards so that their demands on their citizens may be tempered and controlled. For certainly we cannot eliminate the evils of sovereignty by stretching its range until it encompasses the whole of the human race; but we can have in the United Nations the main organ that checks the arbitrariness of governments with inescapable responsibilities and interdependencies.

A large number of the people of the United Nations still enjoy no appreciable measure of political freedom. Yet politics at this highest of its levels makes the expansion of political freedom irrepressible. Unfree nations have entered into an association that has purposes far beyond the understanding and intelligence of their rulers. Because of this organization the preservation or the rebirth of freedom in some countries benefits also peoples who are not yet free. Because of the United Nations, the fact that there are unfree orders can become bearable, and a process of correction is set in motion. We can afford a certain amount of totalitarianism in our world, if we of the democracies do our job of setting and keeping the standards of political freedom. For freedom is so contagious that it can permeate the hard shell of totalitarian regimes, reach their citizens and give them hope.

CHAPTER V

THE SCIENCE OF POLITICS

T HERE IS a new politics as there is a new world. Yet we
find it difficult to recognize the laws of the new politics
or the features of the new world; we complain that they
are not new enough to satisfy our recurrent dreams of
safe, steady progress. Actually, the only thing that seems
to be still unscathed in the world that is being consumed
is our idea of it, to which we desperately cling as if it
were the only world we could conceive of.

We are so accustomed to thinking of a political organization in terms of our own institutions of government,
with their legislature and executive, army and police force,
that we can't seem to reconcile ourselves to the idea that
the new highest sphere of politics might have perspectives
and institutions of its own. Relying on a continual progress
that should take us from need to plenty, from fear to
security, from national to world government, our conception of progress is that of a constant and steady motion.
But constant, steady motion is a form of static equilibrium,
or at least it appears so to those who live it.

Somehow, we have forgotten that motion can be full
of unexpected jolts, varying according to the character of

the moving body and the substance in which the movement occurs. Some of us seem to think of jolts as scandals,
scandals that are regrettable and that one day, we hope,
will give place to an ever-normal steadiness. Others are
attracted by the idea of the one jolt that will end all jolts.
Revolution, it is called. For intellectuals there seems to be
no better course than to decide which among the many
announced revolutions is the one on whose wave it is safe
to ride.

The function of intellectuals is to work with ideas, to
produce or to check or to retail them. There is nothing
magical about ideas. They permit us to visualize within
their own range the world we live in, just as a lens, by
multiplying the power of our eyes, permits us to observe
segments of reality that lie beyond the range of our immediate vision.

Thinking is a type of work and, if well done, makes us
free. Like every other type of work, it can make or unmake us. When it is well done, it helps us make the best
of ourselves, it gives us a field of endeavor proportional
to our strength and the means to increase our strength.
It becomes a medium of communication and mutual understanding with men who spend their energies on other
types of work. It gives us a power related to the circumstances by which it has been prompted.

The test of good thinking is its capability of being trans-
posed to other circumstances and of containing in itself
a corrective of its own faults and limitations. Good thinking is communicable and extendable, it is linked with the
good thinking that has been prompted by different circumstances and establishes with it a relationship, a con-
tinuity. It is an essential sustaining element of civilization.
Well-done thinking is rooted in its times, tied to their

conditions, and at the same time fills the cracks between varying times and conditions.

The name of good thinking is truth, the peculiar kind of power produced by good intellectual work. Truth is never achieved in toto or possessed unconditionally, because truth is the hard-won, liberating proportion of our mind with certain specific facts.

Our attitude toward political ideas is only an instance of our attitude toward ideas, and our attitude toward ideas is only an instance of our attitude toward our work. We have acquired the habit of gliding on our ideas, rather than keeping them under control; of letting them drift, rather than using each of them according to its particular range. But thinking, political or otherwise, is not a joyride. Its function is to establish a working relationship between individuals and the social realities that surround them, a proportion exemplified and embodied in the individual thinker, who guarantees with his person and reputation the social risk his stand entails.

Ideas are of doubtful value unless they suggest modes of action that are respectful of facts and can make inroads on facts to the end of achieving our purposes. When political thinking is well done, the truth it produces creates a dynamic relationship between man and the society around him—a relationship wherein the individual respects the limits imposed on his work, finds room for his work and hope and purpose in his doing. Good political thinking is never a teacher of despair or of action for action's sake. It is never the work of men who make themselves mouthpieces of hopelessness or necessity.

We have made of each of our organized systematic blocks of ideas—or ideologies, as we call them—robots that are meant to sweep everywhere, each sounding the call for its own brand of necessity. Whether it is the philosophy of socialism or the defense of the absolute value of private property, each is assumed to be a panacea of unlimited application. Neither leaves room for choice; each is strong-armed by "either/or," roughened by "or else." We have made an art of not speaking for ourselves when we suggest policies: we pronounce ourselves carriers or transmitters of something above us which speaks through us. Increasingly, the art of thinking has become one of smoothing and polishing up the inevitable.

Perhaps the most dangerous of our fallacies has been our miscalculation of politics, our tendency to assume that a day might come when we could do away with politics. At the same time, in order to bring about that day, politics has been charged with the realization of absolutes. Yet the function of politics is both essential and limited. It cannot be delegated to the automatism of production or law, nor can it accomplish miracles. But somehow we have never been convinced either of the essential or of the limited role politics plays.

In the early days of the modern state, Machiavelli offered an outstanding example of well-done political thinking. By sharply focusing his mind on the facts of his time in his country, he discerned the marks that the energy of man could leave on them. Machiavelli's thought established an operating perspective on these facts, a classical proportion of hard-headed obedience to them and risky action upon them. He told how the fears and hopes of his countrymen could be quickly molded, so that on the habits thus established a strong Italian state could rest.

Into the static political thinking of his time—which consisted of mere classification of types of government and their mutation from one to another—Machiavelli introduced one entirely new element: the interplay between the trends of history and the individual who knows them and purposefully acts on them. He made political thinking three-dimensional and laid down the foundations for the modern science of politics. Yet his science of politics, precise as it was in its rules of operation, was concerned only with the actions of the few professional manipulators of history, and the worth of these actions was determined only by their success. His was a world as lean and sharp as his face. His was the first attempt to snap pictures of men in action against the moving background of history.

It was a crude, primitive, and yet vital conception of politics, suited to the primitive conditions of political civilization in the age before industrialism brought the masses to the foreground. Only the few political protagonists had rights in Machiavelli's time, but now the people are the protagonists and the people have rights.

Machiavelli had only past history to rely on when he wanted to show his principles in operation. Now we have something entirely new: the simultaneous unfolding of political principles, with all their variations, somewhere in the world and the simultaneous payment for mistaken principles by the people everywhere in the world. Political patterns, following the trail that industrialism blazed, circle the globe with extraordinary speed and, in their various adaptations, explode their potentialities. We do not need to consult Roman history now if we want to see a political principle in operation. It is enough to look at a map, supplemented by a newsreel.

In our time we cannot afford to use evil for the noble purpose of national reconstruction. Evil has become both too unsafe and too costly. We have seen what happened to the Italians when belatedly they had their Prince.

The ruthless establishment of industrialism in eighteenth-century England proved safe and profitable to the English at a time when each nation was an isolated world in itself. But now there is no nation big enough or small enough to absorb within its boundaries the impact of its own social experiments. Today the leaders of Soviet Russia, in their ruthless drive toward industrialization, must of necessity accompany the planned isolation of Russia with the planned cruelty of slave labor and a constant stress on war economy—a condition of things that does not contribute to keeping the world at ease.

Our civilization has lost most of the elements that used to provide at least partial or local immunity to evil. Forces may now be set in motion that if unchecked at their source cannot be counteracted. We seemed to have been struck by this fearful realization only after the blast of Hiroshima. But the atomic bomb—this weapon against which we have no defense—merely dramatizes a fact which is perhaps the essential characteristic of our day: we have no defense against any power—be it physical or political—that gets out of control and falls into the hands of evil men. In the new dimensions of our world, compacts with evil have long ceased to be profitable.

Yet, in our habits and patterns of political thinking, we seem still to be with Machiavelli, and frequently far behind him. We have become quite skillful in discovering trends of history but quite shy in singling out spots and occasions where we can operate on them.

When we are disturbed by things that do not conform to patterns, we usually recover our poise by concluding that what contradicts our theories is irrational. Then we either register a protest against irrationality, or we flirt with it.

When we want to appear realistic, we see politics only as the art of getting, not of doing. It is as if in our political thinking we had managed to concentrate all our efforts on either obedience or independence: the unconditional obedience of the self-appointed *fonctionnaires* of history, or the unconditional independence of the footloose uprooted intellectual.

The intellectuals communicate with one another through their ideological shorthand and talk to one another in their own conceited Esperanto. They are always inclined to think that the great languages of the world are vulgarized translations of their Esperanto. During this war which was fought in an ideological vacuum, the manipulators or the retailers of ideas were largely out of work. Now they may come into the open because there is a world that is being made safe for them. If its new dimensions are to be measured and its realities encompassed, their craft is needed.

Ours is a many-dimensional, increasingly balanced, compensated and creative world. It is a world where, on every side, we are discovering boundaries; and where, in a tumultuous process, new checks are being set on the savage independence of nations in the international community and on individuals within their states. It is a finite world, each of whose parts owes its existence to the whole, to which it is bound by an ever-increasing number of ties and dependencies.

The limitation of the scope of internal politics that used to be entrusted to dynasties or constitutions, today is guaranteed by the realities of international life. The limitation of the scope of international politics that used to be entrusted to the niceties of diplomacy, today is achieved by functional international agencies and by the communists or Catholic or socialist "internationals."

In our time mutually binding responsibilities are being established, great power lines are being knotted that used to hang loose. There is the responsibility of governments to their peoples and to the international community. There is the responsibility of business structures to political institutions and of political institutions to business structures. There is the responsibility of ideologies to those sections of reality and those groups of human beings they pretend to reflect or to guide. And there is the responsibility of the manipulator of ideas, a responsibility not discharged simply by announcing or denouncing inevitable trends.

Of these so-called inevitable trends communism is the one now most widely heralded; the one that represents the greatest danger to our freedom, both because of the love and the fear it elicits. It is also the greatest concentration of evil in our time, of evil conditions that are assiduously cultivated by men who are in sympathy with evil.

However, it is our evil; we have called it upon ourselves. It is not, like fascism, a mad secession from civilization, but a long-drawn projection of it—literally our shadow, the bitter outcome of our bad conscience and our bad thinking. It represents the most old-fashioned way of thinking, with its unprincipled Machiavellianism, its blindness to the new realities of international life, its dull repetition of clichés, its exasperating mimicry of democratic institutions and modes of expression.

But we deserve it. Democracy proved incapable of accompanying industrialism in countries whose connection with Western civilization was tenuous. Even in the great Western countries themselves, the masses that capitalism uprooted are not yet absorbed into the life of their commonwealths. In the countries where the reservoirs of rights were shallow, representative institutions were unable to mitigate the terrific uprootings, the shiftings of populations, the upsets in modes of living, that industrialism brings in its train. We cannot complain if the weakness of our political condition reflects the weakness of our thinking.

Not only do we deserve communism but we need it. It shows us the advantage of seeing things in perspective, in terms of a goal, even if the goal reflects a hopelessly wrong conception of society. We need communism as long as people who claim to care for civil liberties continue to make an idol of each right and attribute wondrous qualities to any one of the political institutions of freedom, like elections, party politics or national independence.

We will go on needing communism until we realize that a misconception aggressively pursued is always likely to overshadow a truth dimmed by complacent smugness; and that between perspective thinking and flat, two-dimensional thinking, the former is always bound to win.

In our time a common denominator for all men has been established by the rude facts of economics and technology. These facts both potentially endanger and potentially strengthen that other common denominator which five thousand years of Judaism and Christianity had determined.

Today it is extremely hazardous to countenance a Cesare Borgia, for he is likely to run amok and destroy the world, as Hitler nearly did. Our margin of political error has been sharply reduced, for we can afford only as much evil as we can outweigh. In every part of the world and in the world as a whole, politics has become interdependent in its structure and finite in its scope. Because of this interdependence and this finiteness, it is possible firmly to establish a science of politics in our world.

We can have a science of politics now, because we can see that politics performs an essential function, yet a limited one. It is not the science of power: it is the science of freedom. It is a science not of means that may be weighed with spurious objectivity, but of an overriding goal. We can have a science of politics when we reject the fallacy of boundlessness—be it the boundless power of the individual or of the sovereign state—and the illusion that a permanent, self-adjustable political order can ever be reached.

Politics works now in a world-wide setting and affects all human beings regardless of race, creed or political belief. The patrimony of rights and the reservoir of skills that a nation enjoys react on other nations and affect their people, just as a national deficiency of rights and skills creates a vacuum, a pocket of disturbance, that can affect the world.

The political balance sheet of our interdependent world is not a copy of the economic balance sheet but an integration of it and a compensation for it. Thus the political freedom of some nations is a compensation for the political strictures that other nations still have to endure. In its new world-wide dimension, politics acts as it has always acted in more restricted frameworks.

Strange things are happening. Today the United States, the nation economically and technologically the most advanced, is the one under the heaviest political indebtedness to the rest of the world. Conversely, Soviet Russia, a nation still so backward that it confers on its people a miserably low standard of leisure and comfort, is the most ambitious and aggressive political creditor. The new sphere of worldwide politics, where the two leading nations are at opposite poles, is not conducive to an all-leveling political uniformity but to a wide, measurable range of difference. Its main guarantees are two: variety in political systems, which tends to counteract the monopolistic, leveling trend of economics, and constant effort on the part of the democratic nations to set the highest possible standards of political freedom.

It is this condition of things that has created the United Nations, the clearing house for all political compensations, the center where the creditor pays his debts, the debtor advances his credits, and where political strength is bound to be distributed according to a ratio other than that of sheer economic or military power. The UN owes its existence to the same causes that have made possible a science of politics. Indeed, it bears witness to the imperative need for such a science.

A science of politics, based on an understanding of the scope and the limits of politics, can determine how and under what conditions the major ruptures of freedom occur. It can also prescribe the criteria for the building and the upkeep of the reservoirs of rights. As the technical science of freedom, it will allow us to escape the twofold danger of wholesale dogmatism and unprincipled relativism. It need not be divorced from morality nor limited to a consideration of the economic half of the cycle of human production. It cannot be noncommittal as between good and evil, fascism and democracy; nor can it afford to be indifferent to communism, since it must still make use of it and fight it.

A science of politics can give us tools with which to serve truth and justice under the specific conditions of our own commonwealth and in the larger society of all men. It need not, however, harp on the inescapable reality of these great ideas, nor bear witness to even higher ones, for they can best be served by showing how they work and by making them work. Were they figments of our imagination, nothing would have meaning.

It is a great adult world we are being ushered into, one which can give men an unprecedented, ever-increasing enjoyment of political freedom, equalled only by the economic well-being that is within their reach. It is a world where, for all the complexity and confusion of political phenomena, politics at times acquires an extraordinary degree of elementary clarity—as when the fate of the English nation becomes dependent on the capacity of every citizen to do enough work to keep himself and his commonwealth free.

The mist of ideologies cannot befog the clear outlines that the hierarchy of politics has acquired in our world, a hierarchy starting at the ground floor with the organization of labor, going on to the territorial national level and finally to the international sphere. Within this hierarchy, each political organization can compensate or cheat men for their work as it directs their work. Every attempt to stop at one of the three levels of politics, or to skip any one of them, is invariably wrong: we cannot have politics all centered on the workers' Soviets or on nationalism or on world government, just as we cannot have politics all aimed at crippling trade unions, or national independence or the United Nations.

Ours is not any longer the lean, three-dimensional world of Machiavelli. In our days the knowledge of history is not any more the half-esoteric patrimony of experts who stealthily offer to a single man, prince or would-be prince, the benefit of their advice. Now history can be seen all unfolded: what it does, who makes it, who pays for it. The protagonist of history is not any longer the hero, the great gambler or the great doer. Now we can see everywhere the individual as the maker of history, the one who settles its accounts, and has the irrepressible right to enjoy all the rights he can earn.

Our world does not allow the search after boundless absolutes or monstrous totalitarianisms, yet it depends entirely on the constant production of this sparkle of absolute energy that is freedom. The organization of freedom is increasingly complex; yet its final results, its achievements and failures, are to be seen and felt by everybody. For all its complexities, ours is a transparent, manageable world. It is driven by one type of energy of which there is only one generator; it can follow a course that has a limited range of alternatives, and all radical deviations from this course, all mistakes in the release or in the conservation of this energy, are exceedingly costly. Recent history has proved how disastrous are all attempts to drive the society of men with any other type of energy, like the unleashed power of the political or technological machines, and how the power of freedom is the only one that is safe for men to use, for it is the only one that is not self-destructive.

The knowledge of the absolute value of freedom, of the laws of its release and use, can guide us to find the specific jobs that are to be done and that can be done. We must establish according to entirely new lines the range of privacy and of interdependence both for individuals and for nations; we must gradually eliminate the causes that still make for clusters of tyranny and crying injustice in our times. From the awareness of both the finiteness and the univocal direction of our world, we can derive all the strength we need.

Ours is a four-dimensional, precariously balanced, finite and measurable world. It is a terrifying world. Yet men have the capacity and can increasingly acquire the knowledge to run it. It does not promise to be a world of total peace or rest. But it is a world where even strife and struggle give men the opportunity to increase the power and to control the course of the freedom they make.